Re:Un

A contemporary journey
in Christian mysticism

Anina Thomas

GILEAD
B O O K S
PUBLISHING

Gilead Books Publishing
Corner Farm
West Knapton
Malton
North Yorkshire, YO17 8JB, UK
First published in Great Britain, June 2014
2 4 6 8 10 9 7 5 3 1

British Library Cataloguing-in-Publication Data:
A catalogue record for this book is available from the British Library.

ISBN-13: 978-0-9926713-4-1

The publisher makes every effort to ensure that the papers used in
our books are made from trees that have been legally sourced from
well-managed and credibly certified forests by using a printer
awarded FSC & PEFC chain of custody certification.

Editor: Matt Bradburn
Cover photograph by Matthew Reeve
With thanks to Stephen Broadbent and Chester Cathedral for
permission to use an image of the *Water of Life* sculpture
Cover design: Nathan Ward

This book is dedicated to my beautiful Jesus, my loving Father and my friend, Holy Spirit.

All things come from you,
and of your own do we give you.[1]

Contents

Acknowledgements

Thanks to my brave, adventurer, husband Gaz and my precious, free-spirited, warrior daughter Winnie. A 'selah' and a 'yamas!' as we continue on this adventure together.

Thanks to all those who study and have worked at the Light Project: Chris, Glyn, Melly, Dezzer, Gareth and Phoebe. You have taught me to keep the main thing the main thing and have shown me community, accepted me and afforded me space. This is priceless.

Thanks to those pioneers who keep journeying—no matter what the cost—to discover the pasture of open spaces for generations to come. Gill, walking with you has taught me so much.

Thanks to the intercessors whose hidden faithful lives reveal the reality of the kingdom of God. Pam, thank you for our journey in prayer together.

Thanks to the mystics, martyrs, prophets, revivalists and desert dwellers: such richness! Misunderstood by many, but intimate with God. Thanks to those with wasted, beautiful kingdom lives.

Misty, the Helsers, Mother Theresa and Heidi Baker, Bob and Pam, you inspire me.

Thanks to my Jesus-loving buddies, my long-distance scattered community and those who have encouraged me on this journey: 271 Western Roaders, old St Michael's buddies, New Wine conferences, Worship Academy, Phil and Mags, team Pitt, Aliss, Ju, Bob, Matt 'n' Meg, Josh and Lucy, Nancy and the Stevies, Justin and Jane.

Thank you to Chris Hayes at Gilead for publishing this book, taking risks and following the nudges of the Holy Spirit. Matt Bradburn also gets a special mention for editing; what a great combination of skill and God-honouring.

Thanks to those who have tried to help but whom I have frustrated much. I release and bless those who haven't understood. Thanks for walking with me awhile.

Thanks to my family, Mum Dad and Tania. You kept me safe and showed me what graft, generosity, loyalty and dedication look like.

Introduction

I was brought up in a traditional, middle class home with my younger sister and dedicated Mum. My much-loved Father was away as a sea captain for the majority of the time. We went to church and I wanted to be good but I had never met Jesus or even heard rumours of the beautiful Holy Spirit. I felt different to everyone else, like I didn't fit in anywhere, but I experienced the focused burning power of love, belonging and acceptance (a foretaste!) through the gift of music, my wonderful Scottish granny and my fledgling relationship with my later husband-to-be. I know some of my school teachers prayed for me and I was confirmed as a teenager, which added to the great background of knowledge about God I already had.

The Lord finally burst onto my page when I was a university student; unhappy, unfulfilled and on a path of self-destruction. I was staying with my boyfriend (now my husband) at his student house in Sheffield where he was the only atheist in a house full of alive Christians. It was 3am on a Sunday morning and I was suddenly being bathed in the unmeasured overwhelming, liquid love of God the Father. I knew this was the God of the Bible and Jesus' father: He was huge and in the room. He saw me, yet He loved me. From that moment on, I was captivated. I made a wholehearted commitment as a new Christian a few hours later, knowing everything would change!

Later that day I met Jesus. It was Sunday and so the students took me to church. It was communion and as people began to go up to the table to receive bread and wine, the enormity of what Jesus did for humanity on the cross hit me and tears streamed down my face in a steady flow for hours. I remember thinking: How can people walk up for communion and not crawl?! I was thoroughly, beautifully, messily undone and managed—I don't know how—to receive communion myself, my heart bursting with gratitude, joy and humility.

The ensuing years have not always been easy. Those who know us as a family will know why. There have been extended periods of such darkness; some done in my own strength, others in a heap at the Cross. I know which were better! Those ten years following our coming to faith were like a vacuum where the Lord just held us. We must have grown in faith but it was imperceptible to us. We were surviving.

Light began to break through after the birth of our daughter. Since then and to the present day, though friendships and the grace of God, I have experienced both incredible emotional healing and His presence in a powerful way. I began to get to know the Holy Spirit personally, dance with Him and yield to Him as a person. I discovered the beauty of repentance and walking with Him daily. I began to learn about prayer, healing, the Father's heart and having adventures in the spirit. He took me deep into the mystical realm and I began to see, travel and visit heaven. I learnt about union with Christ and living in this physical body but allowing the unseen, eternal and supernatural to become a constant reality. I have struggled at times to live in this place whilst simultaneously experiencing the backdrop of the world, superimposed as my so-called life. But I have found that His grace is more than enough for me and the privilege of walking closely with Him in the garden without separation is all my treasure, reward and compensation.

Throughout my journey so far, I have kept journals of my experiences and things He has taught and shown me. I never had the ambition to write a book, but now I sense Him asking me to share some of my treasures. (Passages that are italicised and dated are excerpts from my journals.) I am passionate about signposting the pathway of life for others, leaving people in the presence of God, and awakening the body to reach out to touch those who are lost (whether lost inside the comfort and routine of the building or the system, or lost and drowning at sea, outside of faith) and especially those on the very edges. Without knowing Jesus as a friend, the power and equipping of the Holy Spirit and a relationship in rest with God our father, we are all lost.

I mention this to make it clear that I am an ordinary girl. I don't come from a generational line of "intimates" or a supernatural background. I first met God in my twenties. I had lived a hedonistic life and experienced tough times. I write because I believe that anyone can walk with God and know Him intimately.

This book is a collection of basic teachings to remove barriers to union and some suggestions to help you practice experiencing the depths of God and His presence. It is not supposed to be a heavy theological study so I don't intend to try and justify what I have experienced. If anything you read offends you, confuses you or feels unfamiliar to you by the yardstick of the Bible, ask God what He says and whether it is permissible to you. Some of the things I have seen others do are not for me and I have had to bless those people and walk away. I have also stood nervously on the threshold of something unfamiliar and new, yet knowing that it's right and that once you enter, you'll never be the same again. I pray for wisdom and courage for you to know the difference.

So far I have walked much of this mystical life alone. At first I was ashamed, like it was heresy, and although I loved being drawn deeper into Him, so few people understood that for many years I hid these precious things. I would be frequently alone with God but wouldn't allow the manifestations and secret-place revelations to be seen in community. In time, I began to meet people who were able to explain and give names to what I was experiencing: not only are they OK, but they are gifts to build up the church and turn her outwards. This was such a relief and it has released me into the prophetic and from pretending to 'be normal' with my immediate and church family! Recently I have begun to read about other mystics, prophets, intercessors, revivalists, desert dwellers, pioneers and intimates. They are a great encouragement and feel like old friends.

This book is like a snapshot, the momentary close of a camera shutter that captures the scene early on in my earth-years with God, and it stands still in time. But as the shutter opens, my life in Him continues. I know that what I have experienced is the tip of the iceberg, a tiny dot in the vast spectrum of eternity I have with God. My heart is not to limit, box in or define God's mystery, but to share, encourage and provide a springboard for you in your life with God.

Iranaeus of Lyon was credited as saying, "For the glory of God is a living man; and the life of man consists in beholding God."[2] I cannot say that you will have the same experiences as mine, but I hope you will have many more! My prayer is that you come to know Him fully, are released to express the glory of God however He chooses and that the kingdom and its fruit would abound wherever you move. Glory to Him!

Chapter 1
The Basics

It took me a long time to learn the basics: my hope is that you can learn them quicker than I did! They serve as a foundation for maturity as we grow in wisdom to handle the more supernatural and mystical things of God. They are Biblical, but in my experience, rarely taught or experienced in the Christian community.

Synopsis

Humankind is involved in the most wonderful story ever. The central overarching theme is love. And whether we have come to faith or not, we are all sons made for relationship by and with the God of the universe who is alive, active and passionate about us. Because of Jesus, we are united with God *now*; heaven isn't something reserved for when you die. Once you welcome the King into your heart, the kingdom makes residence in you immediately and all the blessing, authority and reign of God are shared with you. I believe there is a gap in the lives of those who haven't yet met Jesus, which can be either be filled to the brim and overflowing without cost with the nature and character of God himself, or temporarily filled at great personal and spiritual cost with counterfeit fruits and gifts. These can satisfy for a while but will never go deep enough. All the kingdom things of God have opposites, counterfeit but empty alternatives. Instead of the peace, joy and ecstasy of God there are all sorts of substances, highs, stimulants and relaxants. Our fascination with and abuse of image and sex often cover up a desire to be deeply known and loved.

The main characters
God

God is made up of Father, Son and Holy Spirit. As well as them being distinct characters, which means we can get to know them as individuals, they have been inseparable since the beginning of time. There is a circuit of unity, adoration and respect between them; the Father presenting Jesus, Jesus pointing the way to the Father, and the Spirit revealing Jesus to us so that we follow Him and know the Father. We are invited into a big, unending, raucous dance where the circle gets wider and wider the more you become aware of it.

This King has a kingdom which is entirely 'other' to any other kingdom because it is full of the goodness of God and His rule and reign. The advance of this kingdom is not just about the acquisition of souls, but about the whole of creation being redeemed. Jesus has come—and will come again—to bring the whole creation to rights.

We can know God intimately. The first humans were created knowing God and walking with him without shame and without anything getting in the way, living forever in fullness of health and totally satisfied because of Him. This is still His intention for humanity. This means you and me, irrespective of what has happened to you in the past and whatever the future might hold.

You

You are dearly loved by God, made to be with him and with his very presence and life inside you; never to be hungry again for those things outside of Him. You have been made unique, like the beautiful spectrum of colours we see in the palette of creation, existing fully alive, through relationship and for His delight and glory. There is a plan already for your life and when you are born, you are born into a specific time and place with good works to do in those circumstances. He sees you, right now, just as you are. Nothing is hidden from Him, and yet He loves you, with a tidal wave of passion. He wants you to know Him like a best friend, feel Him close and to experience Him and walk with Him. He can forgive anything and heal everything. Nothing is impossible for him. No heart is too shameful or dirty. No one has strayed too far. He has paid the price in full for your ransom and return and that is his gift to you. Do you want your life to truly begin? Are you ready? Just receive.

The world

The world is the backdrop to where we live in the flesh, in our bodies with skin on. There is nothing *inherently* wrong with the world; many aspects of the world echo and agree with how glorious God is. But because of sin, there are some things which are very wrong.

God's 'plan A' was, is and always will be Jesus. He strengthens us to not conform to the 'norm' of what is presented around us, but to live by another standard and by another kingdom. We are not to avoid the world, thinking that to do so keeps us incubated, quarantined and holy, but to overflow and engage in it as God shows us how. The lost, whether they're inside our church buildings, outside on the streets or hidden in the shadows, are those Jesus seeks and draws back home, through His grace and great, triumphing, redeeming love. God is everywhere and in everything, whether we recognise Him or not. This notion is known as 'prevenient grace' and means that we are free to get out of our quarantined church bunkers and find out what He is already doing in our communities.

The ekklesia

The word 'ekklesia' is most commonly used in the Bible to describe those who love God, are yielded to Him and live lives which make Him smile. Living in unity, love, generously with justice and mercy, fruitfulness (with the fruits of the spirit, not necessarily producing huge numbers of salvations and healing), anointing and at rest in Him, His ekklesia is what Jesus is coming back for. They are His beloved, His bride. He is besotted by her and jealous for her. The true ekklesia is a remnant of faithful people. A laid down, yielded, hollowed out, filled up, devoted group of Jesus lovers, free to follow wherever the Holy Spirit tells them to and ravenous for the things of God.

The church

We have got ever so confused! To simply take a building and hold a weekly meeting to sing, study and pray does not necessarily yield ekklesia. Our gathered times (whether in ones and twos, groups in homes or in buildings) are to be a celebration of those things God has been doing. They are a sharing and an equipping for what is next as we connect with God's life together, being ourselves and telling stories of God's activity in the every-day and gossiping Holy Ghost stories. The 'real deal' is control- and religion-free; a family, a community where everyone gets to play.

There is no such thing as the perfect 'church'. We need awakening in those places where we know more *about* God than we actually know Him as a person. We need to stop just telling our children 'stories' about heroes from long ago and begin to be real and encourage them to meet God for themselves. He wants to use everyone just as they are. I don't just seek revival for the body of Christ (an awakening, a refreshing) but society transformation and a habitation, whereby God is pleased to dwell in greater power and presence. The effects are not short-lived, but flow out to all areas and people, 'infecting' relationships and landscapes and maturity and faithfulness as well as tearing down strongholds, reducing crime and addiction and adding numbers to our company.

Satan

Satan, our enemy, was an angel who was created to worship. He was close to God at His throne. satan's beauty and desire to be like God overwhelmed him and he was consumed with pride. Seeing as nothing evil or contrary to the nature of God is allowed in His kingdom, satan was thrown out of heaven, along with many other corrupted angels, to eternal punishment in hell. Hell is not satan's kingdom or place of power or stronghold. He is weak and only allowed to do what he has permission to do. He is like an animal who has been disarmed with claws and teeth pulled out. He can have power, but only when we give it to him. In fact, God showed me once that satan is like the Wizard of Oz; a small being, who projects himself as larger than he actually is.

Satan rules through fear, lies and accusation. If we are feeling accused, allowing fear to control our thoughts and actions or believing and acting on the opposite to what God says about ourselves, others or Himself, we have believed one of satan's lies. All are his trademarks, but the good news is that once we have received Jesus into our lives, satan cannot get into our space. He can only whisper or shout from the other side of the door. It's like a door where the handle is on our side and we can choose whether to let him in or not.

Because of Jesus's powerful and sinless death, resurrection and ascension, He has overcome all death and sickness and sin in our place, so when satan accuses us, we just remind him of our place with Christ and tell him to get lost. Walking in union with God helps us recognise when we might have opened the door to satan and given him access, but we can quickly come back to God, say we are sorry, receive forgiveness, reject our enemy and turn in the opposite direction.

Satan can see what we are doing, but cannot tell what we are thinking. This is a useful thing to remember as we pray and increase in sensitivity to Gods prompting to sometimes pray wordlessly.

Just one thing...

New Christians can get quite bogged down with all the new 'rules' and things to get to grips with. They can often feel very defeated and disillusioned. No wonder! I wish someone had told me in the early days that I just needed to enjoy relationship with God, listening to His voice and enjoying His company! Seeking Him and spending time with Him is the answer to everything. You'll find you begin to prefer His ways more and your choices will become those which please Him anyway.

We often get our knickers in a twist with questions like: "How do I know what God is saying to me?", "Should I go out with Person-X?", "Does God want me to take that job?" and so on. Loving Him and learning to recognise His voice is all you need to know. His grace is wide enough that we can make mistakes and He forgives us. Reading the Bible whilst inviting the Holy Spirit to inspire our understanding, seeking advice from others, going to church, praying, giving, evangelism and so on can all be good, but none of these is a substitute for authentic relationship with God. If we don't know Him, they are empty and religious. Love the Lord with all your heart and give Him everything you've got; seek first the Kingdom, and everything else will flow. What you behold will determine what you become.

Chapter 2
Freedom

God's original design for humankind was to walk with Him without shame and in freedom. The walk Adam enjoyed in the garden, knowing the Lord and strolling with Him in full rest in the shade of the day; this is what we have been created for. Once you experience true freedom, you never want to return to bondage or slavery again. The process of freedom can happen in an instant or sometimes God walks us through it, step by step. We can ask God to set us free from anything which holds us back and prevents us from being fully who we were created to be. We can invite the Spirit of truth to shine His light on anything which opposes freedom. If you dare, invite the fire of God to come and purify you, so your desires are aligned with His and space is made in your thoughts, heart, body, spirit and soul to love Him unreservedly.

Here are some barriers to freedom. There can be a variety of causes, including heredity (being passed down the family line) or trauma. It's easy to feel overwhelmed by our issues, that they are too deep rooted, too long lasting or too difficult to be free from, but that is just a lie from the enemy to keep you familiar with these issues or allow them to become false comforts. Whatever they are, they are all covered by Jesus' universal, over-arching and complete work on the cross and you can invite God to deal with them in your life. The Holy Spirit will show you how, whether through taking authority, inner or emotional healing, forgiveness, repentance or perhaps deliverance. Allow the Holy Spirit to lead in this. If it feels too much of a hurdle to jump on your own, perhaps ask someone to pray with you. He can prompt the other person to help you navigate through any uncharted waters!

Lies

Knowing the truth of who we are is really important. The world wants to squeeze you into its mould and the enemy, the father of lies, wants to mislead you. The truth is that we are beloved children of God who, from a place of rest, can exert the reality of the Kingdom of God on earth. We have authority because of Jesus's death and resurrection and we are His children. This means we can drive out demons, heal every disease and nullify the plans of the enemy so that nothing will harm us. The enemy seeks to undermine our identity as sons, and when we believe his lies and adopt mind-sets which are from our old nature, we begin to align ourselves and agree with him. God can reveal to us any lies that are rooted in our subconscious, way back and buried deep down, as nothing is hidden from Him.

Vows

Vows are promises we make. As we speak, our words have power to bless or curse. When we speak words that come into agreement with God, we are effectively saying, "Amen!" and are in alignment with His will. However, if we say something about a situation or a person or ourselves which is not truth, we are coming into agreement with the enemy. This gives him a power which can become a stronghold, or a place of power in us. If we have done this, consciously or not, we can simply say sorry and begin to walk in the opposite way, focused on being a blessing, speaking truth and hope and life, motivated by love.

Inadvertently I made a vow in my early 20s which became a stronghold for a good ten years afterwards. It happened out of pain and an inability to cope well with my circumstances. I remember making the decision, "I am never going to let anyone see my hurt again. I will not be weak. I will not cry." This became my vow; I vaguely recall even now saying it aloud, and for many years, I did not cry, I did not feel and it seemed to keep the pain at bay.

Years later, my prayer partner told me about a mutual friend who was pregnant and whose babies were at risk. My response was curt, bitter and matter-of-fact, lacking in compassion or empathy. I had lost the ability to feel. I was numb and in that moment, I knew it was wrong.

Soon afterwards, I began to attend 'Worship Academy', a course for those involved in leading worship. I experienced God's heavy, inhabiting presence for the first time; His overwhelming love, reassuring touch, deep searching eyes and His invitation to wholeness. I was undone, mascara all over my face; God had come close. Over a period of twelve weekends, God dealt with everything. He reassured me of His constant love and tender father's care. It was as though He sat me down and invited me to get the next thing off the dusty shelf I had put away out of reach, one after another, and we looked at it together. For each incident, He took me deep into each memory and showed me that He was right there with me. I acknowledged the pain and the raw emotions and then asked him to heal, which included the Holy Spirit showing me how to forgive and release fully. I was being set free.

Control

Something God really also had to free me from was control. From a young age, I wanted to 'be good' and learnt that showing emotion was negative. Without the proximity of my Sea Captain father, I sought the attention of the opposite sex to answer that question that most young girls have: 'Am I pretty?' From the age of about 14, I controlled food and began to experiment with alcohol and drugs to numb my sense of not fitting in at school. At University, I added exercise and cigarettes to my list of addictions, took anti-depressants and hid behind characters and manipulated listeners whilst studying music as a soloist. Into this mess I was newly born as a Christian, and immediately, difficult and hectic life circumstances forced me in the role of carer which I reluctantly took. All at once, many things were outside my control. I learnt slowly that God was a safe place and if I released my tightly clenched fist, He could take those painful and harmful things and bring truth, healing, peace and rest. You can't have both control and peace; they don't sit together. If you are aware that you control people, situations, food, substances, sleep, circumstances, emotions and you feel distanced from people and numb, it may be time to invite God in and release your tight grip.

False responsibility

A close relative to control is 'false responsibility' and it encourages you to carry a weight or load which does not belong to you. This can result in people finding it difficult to say no when asked to help and feeling an ungodly burden towards people, relationships, situations and the workplace.

I often tried to play God in the early days and got exhausted! Often the reason was that I believed a lie about His nature, and felt that it wouldn't harm to put both our heads together and double the effort, especially when I got impatient with His timing! However, knowing truth sets you free. He is good, He cares and intends to bless. I can't make anyone happy or keep them well. I can't fix any situation or make people whole. I can't save people and I can't make them believe in God. It is important to relinquish false responsibility and learn how to release everything to the God who cares and never sleeps. This means we can enter into deep rest and know that ultimately, everything will be okay. We do our job and let God do His.

The Biblical picture of the oxen and the yoke is helpful here. Each ox had a neck piece especially made to fit them which was not too heavy or cumbersome. As they walked in step with the plough, the yoke was light. If one tried to pull his own way, the pressure of the load would be so uncomfortable that he would come back in line and be relieved of the burden. Walking in step with God and only doing what God asks us to makes our journey much more pleasurable! This gives you permission, when asked to do something new, to accept if God has already given you the green light, say no if God has already indicated that it is not the best for you, or to buy yourself time to hear God's best by simply saying "Thank you for asking me. I'm going to go away and pray about that."

Rebellion

It's easy to think of rebellion as something that is concerned only with major issues resulting in off-the-scale acts of disobedience, such as the prodigal son, Jonah, Lot's wife or modern-day church leaders who 'fall' spectacularly.

However, rebellion is simply defined as critical thinking, speaking or behaviour towards those in authority over you. Rebellion isn't just manifested in obvious moral failures, but in subtleties such as personal preferences, or what we mistakenly begin to feel are our entitlements; those things we feel we are owed, such as our time, our comforts, our appearance, our money, our service, our emotions, our rewards or recognitions. This arises from a sort of spiritual 'tithing' of those things we feel are our rights. This reveals that there are areas in our life which are not submitted to God, which is rebellion.

As the *ekklesia*, we need to be careful how we behave towards those in authority and make sure we foster a culture of honouring, gratitude and of blessing one another. We need to be aware that the Spirit of Christ will appear how and when He chooses and not just in the forms we expect, the musical worship styles we prefer or in the holy places and righteous people we expect! God will be God. How many times have we passed judgement when we have seen the Spirit move in ways that we are not familiar with? He seems to deliberately avoid patterns in His guises and appearances when He decides to visit. He is the same foretold Messiah who arrived in diapers and in weakness and humanity, the One who sees and welcomes hunger in the messy love-act of a visiting prostitute, who tells the expert fishermen that the catch is on the opposite side of the boat to where they were expecting, who speaks in intimacy and revelation to an estranged and sinful woman in the heat of the day yet does not utter a word in court before the honoured dignitaries. This is the same One who is found wherever He will be made truly welcome, who may turn up anywhere at any time and instantly offend us as He touches down amongst the homeless, or the established church, or anywhere else we least expect Him to be.

The opposite of rebellion is submission to those in authority over us, as it expresses a faith in God's ultimate authority. This can get complicated, especially when those in authority no longer hold to what we might consider to be gospel issues. This often makes me think about the two generations of Israelites in the desert, those who grumbled and lingered there forty years longer than perhaps necessary, and those who entered the Promised Land. If you are struggling to belong in the community where you are worshipping, do not stay and grumble, but attempt to address issues directly with leadership. If you are unable to submit, then sometimes it may be necessary to leave and move on, blessing them in your heart and leaving without causing any division. Sometimes this really tests our character, but our God has equipped us and our lives are no longer our own. We give up our entitlements to reputation, being seen as right or being honoured in the sight of men, but instead walk humbly and obediently with God.

God appears to be doing something new within the *ekklesia*; whilst continuing to move amongst those established groups who seek Him, He is calling a remnant, an exiled people closer to His heart. Perhaps you cannot belong to the established church, yet you long for belonging. You may have been reading in Acts about simple organic fellowship and long for a less cluttered, less labour-intensive way to meet in community. You may have been looking for what you have sensed and seen in the Spirit, yet it is no-where to be found locally or nationally yet. Don't lose heart if this is the case. I know many at present whose 'holy discontent' and longing for more Jesus-focused freedom and authenticity is forging something new. The main thing is to continue relationship with God and others and trust that He is making a way. He is so good at doing that.

Repentance and forgiveness

Repentance is a beautiful gift that restores us back to God. It breaks the connection to our old nature and the way of death. When we repent of sin, it breaks the enemy's hold over our lives and restores us to full peace in God. We simply invite God to reveal our heart, shine His light and then we swiftly deal with our sin, without needing to hang around and camp in guilt and shame! Thank God that because of Jesus, we no longer need sackcloth and ashes or drawn-out self-flagellation. Neither do we need to get stuck in the 'sin-repent' cycle, because true repentance (*metanoia*) is a fundamental renewing of our minds. All that is needed is for the signed, sealed and delivered union which was bought and paid for in full, thousands of years ago on a cross, is a grateful heart, ready to receive.

There are many misconceptions, especially in Christian circles, about forgiveness. Firstly there is a lot of shame attached to repentance and we forget the truth that it is God's kindness that leads us to repent. We have a very good Father with nothing but love in His eyes, patiently waiting for us to turn back to Him, ready to swoop us up into the air. He forgets our deeds as soon as they are mentioned.

I like to think about the instant and complete nature of forgiveness like this: The enemy comes to God and says, "So, what about Anina? Did you see what she did? Look!" to which God says, "I don't know what you are talking about!" Because of the cross and its completion and absolute resolution, because He sees me through the lens of Jesus, the righteous One, all evidence has been destroyed. It is finished! Sin and death and my old self have no hold any more. The relief inside, the gratitude from being free, the rush of acceptance and the rest and peace that comes from repentance is beautiful. It costs us nothing except pride and it cost Him everything.

An indication that we need to repent is when we lose peace or take offence easily. Guilt can also keep us locked in unforgiveness. Sometimes people choose, consciously or subconsciously, to keep a hold onto unforgiveness as they mistakenly believe that the other person who has perpetrated our pain is being punished and made to feel the same hurt and pain as they are. This is futile as it does not hurt the other person but imprisons us as bitterness takes hold.

I recently became aware that the Lord was putting his finger on an area where I had judged the church. I was resisting repentance and the battle of wills intensified because I didn't want to submit to God. Pride and self-righteousness had me in a tug of war: I was like a stubborn horse, stopping abruptly before a hurdle! But the Lord just waited.

Eventually, in my friend's living room, I got up from the sofa and knelt on the carpet. It was a first step towards humility; a relenting, a death to self and pride. After that, repentance quickly flowed and I was then overwhelmed by a revelation of the true state of my heart. I was able to fully say sorry. As I lingered, He revealed more hidden motives of my heart, and until there was nothing left but a yielded, happy heart and deep rest. Repentance is not a feeling, but a decision and an act of the will.

Recently, I have come to understand that when our prayers are effectively saying, 'Change that person' or 'Oh God, please deal with that pride over there', we are heading for revelation of our own hardness of heart and heaping judgement on ourselves. Learning to walk lightly with God means ceasing to look critically at everyone and everything which does not align to our way and humbly walking with our eyes on the Lord, one step at a time. Only He can convict of sin and He will do it when He chooses. When we play God, we are only getting in the way!

Emotional Healing

In God's hands, we are safe. Emotional healing is when God brings us healing from previous hurts, pain, memories, opposition, traumas and wounding. His healing is wonderfully thorough. He does not pull out weeds by just tugging at the leaves; he gets to the bottom of the issue, uprooting it and destroying it completely, so the weed never grows again. We don't know how long emotional healing will take. Sometimes it feels painful, with us very aware of the process and maybe having to forgive people and release memories and events. At other times, God does a very deep work, spirit to spirit, rather like being operated on whilst unconscious, and it's only afterwards that we realise we are healed and free. Either way, we can feel afterwards like we have gone through the wringer or like we need intensive care after an operation.

In my experience, I needed to take some time quietly, without lots of people and noise around, and almost in a foetal state, go back to ensuring I had only my basic needs met. I found I tended to dress in comfy slobby clothes, wrap up warm, cancel visitors, eat nourishing food and get lots of sleep. You can feel overwhelmed and drained and so allowing some space to let everything sink in and be totally restored by God is very necessary. After Jesus' extended time in the wilderness, angels came to tend him. I often muse on what they actually did, or brought Him! If Jesus needed restoration following this difficult time, then surely we do too.

Faking it

At first, it is easy to think that as no one truly sees what is going on inside, you can fake it, especially if you're carrying pain. Fake religion, fake happiness, fake holiness, fake intimacy and fake manifestations all cause us to put on 'masks', like the clown who pretends not to be feeling sad. But the reality is that deep down you *do* know what's going on. Not only that, but those who walk with God who are gifted in discernment, as well as God himself who sees our heart motives, know as well. The pretence drives distance between ourselves, God and those who would love to help and get to know the 'real us' better. Whilst it is wise not to share all your deepest secrets with everyone—scripture advises us to guard our hearts as that is where life springs up from—to be real with some trusted people is very important. Ask God who is safe to share with.

I have known times where I have wanted so much to fit in that I have imitated what was happening around me for fear of being thought of as less spiritual. My husband remembers faking falling over in the Spirit as everyone before him went down and he didn't know it was okay to stay on your feet! There have certainly been times when I have hidden my sadness or pretended everything was alright on the outside, when inside I felt like I was falling apart. My diagnosis for post-natal depression came six months following my daughter's birth and because I felt so ashamed that I wasn't coping, I pretended to everyone who visited or offered help that I was doing well.

A turning point came as a friend prayed for me in 2005. It was one of the most gutting experiences because God revealed to her how my relationship with Him, ten years post-commitment, was still rather fledgling. People knew me as a worship leader, a youth leader, a vicar's-wife-to-be and someone who seemed to have life sorted. But this was *God's* word. He sees deep within us and knows us better than we know ourselves: "I am taking the shell of this relationship and shattering to smithereens your fear of getting it wrong and trying to please Me and be good so that you might be loved. You don't need to hide feeling angry any more, dressing everything up and dancing the dance. You will have a relationship with Me like no earthly one you have ever experienced. As a child still, you are constantly looking to be loved and knowing that you are loveable. The child needs to know she is loved."

Walking in freedom

Christ has done for us what we could not do ourselves. Those who have received God and His gift of new life are dead to sin and alive in Him. Walking closely to Him protects us from the attack of the enemy who can't stand the presence and light of God, so the safest and best place for us is on the lap of our Father God. We don't need to fear, but live increasingly aware of His big love and close wonderful presence, enjoying heaven and releasing it wherever we go.

We stay free through surrendered hearts, inspired in us through the Holy Spirit (the clue's in the name!) and standing under the authority of Christ. We know the truth by imbibing it and ruminating on it, allowing scripture to embed within us and give us that unshakeable plumb-line. Don't be like those who just read the words, but inhale deeply, allowing truth to permeate your body, your heart, your mind and your spirit.

The more we walk with the Holy Spirit, the more sensitive we will become to His way for us and the degree to which we stray will shrink. Whilst there are universal doctrines in the Bible, there are other issues which are to be discerned by the individual; permissible to some and not to others. Don't compare yourself to others and get hung up on or offended by what they seem to be able to do, but walk the walk He has called you to. It will result in freedom for you and glory for Him! Having this plumb-line of truth doesn't mean we are immune to temptation and sinning—we may momentarily slip or monumentally fall—but remember that repentance is a beautiful gift. Embrace it and tell the enemy to get lost! satan will try to convince you that your sin is not fully dealt with, but a deft reminder of the power of the cross for total forgiveness, a batting away by letting scripture 'repeat on us' and a focus on Jesus should deal with him!

At first, some of these practices can feel quite foreign and unfamiliar. Commands and encouragements to walk in this way are prolific throughout scripture, but we often presume they are pictorial and not literal. As we operate in this freedom, our reliance will shift from others to God and we will mature as believers fed by His hand. His freedom will become second nature, enabling us to stand, then to walk, then to run and then to fly in Him.

Chapter 3
Hearing the voice of God

Once God had begun to heal me and I was taking my first faltering steps in walking in greater freedom, I noticed that I had become more sensitive to God's voice and His presence. It was as if my ears were opened, I was kissed awake and a whole new world opened itself up to me. His kingdom slowly became my playground.

Some of the things which then accelerated my ability to hear the voice of God were an openness to Him, a desire for Christ as my first love and a recognition of the simple truth that God wants to speak to us all. In the early days, I had the misconception that the voice of God would be like hearing an actual voice and it meant that I wasn't open to Him speaking in other ways. We are promised in scripture that those who know Him and closely follow Him know His voice. We are made in the image of God, but sometimes we mistakenly re-invent Him in ours!

The closer I got to Jesus, I sensed His 'speaking' being more like a scent in the wind, more subtle than I had first imagined, but also more frequent. At first it was fleeting, but it still left me with the impression of knowing something, of having an imprint in my spirit. I would begin to 'know' how other people were feeling deep down, like if the enemy was tormenting them or facts about their lives and hobbies. All of these things were revealed by the Spirit of God and are what we call "words of knowledge". Many times at first, I would ignore or push these 'knowings' away for fear of getting it wrong or being seen as weird. However, as I took risks in acting on what God was saying, I realised that what I was hearing was accurate and had a positive effect on the recipient, and I loved seeing God touch people's lives. The following things may be helpful for you in hearing the voice of God.

Discovering our identity

It is important to know deep down who we are, what our identity is and who we were created to be. This not only gives us purpose and blesses God, oiling our communication with Him, but it also builds the church, prepares the bride and releases the kingdom.

Often in our churches, as in the world, the subtle twist in focus can be on what we do and how we can serve according to our giftings, rather than being released to be who we are. The simplest way to discover this is to ask God! You can do this simply and straightforwardly, or creatively; perhaps waiting and listening for a while afterwards. He may tell you immediately and directly or through others, circumstances, the Bible, emotions, or something you watch or listen to. Often he will confirm it, more so in the early days until we learn for this to be instinctive.

If you wanted to do this creatively, you could gather some art materials, a Bible etc. and begin to draw or write and see what happens. Ask Him questions such as: What do I mean to you? How do you see me? What is my name? In the first years of faith, God sent many people to encourage me with words about who I was and what I was made to be in Him. The same Bible verses kept coming up, the same words. Even though I didn't see it at the time, it began to build up a picture for me retrospectively. For me, these words were often about singing, presence, revival, healing, God's heart, intercession, insight, compassion and power evangelism. God said many times that to Him I am like Mary of Bethany, who will be content to just sit with Him whilst others rush around, doing.

God doesn't want us to get obsessed by what our gifts are. We cannot please Him more by using them well. As we seek Him with all our heart, these things will fall into place without striving. Once, He said this to me:

> *Just give me your heart. I don't want all the stuff you can do; I just want you. I want your heart. If you feel like you have nothing to bring to the table, I want you to know, I don't want what you are going to be or what you think you'd like to be. Just come to me.* (October 2003)

Silence, simplicity and solitude

Going deep with God requires staying still and being relaxed and at rest. There are so many distractions! Like over-stimulated babies, we need to shut out those things which will blunt our sensitivity to the voice of God. As we grow accustomed to His voice, we will become more adept at communing and communicating with him on the run, although whatever stage we are at, God will often whisper His precious invitation for our souls to come away with Him and delight in the richest of fare without cost.

Why spend money on what is not bread, and your labour on what does not satisfy? Listen, listen to me, and eat what is good, and you will delight in the richest of fare. (Isaiah 55:2, NIV)

This seems to be a greater challenge with the increasing advances in technology and the frequency of emails, phone calls, texts, tweets and updates. At work, in leading prayer for students, even holding silence for a minute can seem like an eternity. Constantly 'checking in' with the world can be addictive. So, set time aside with God but be realistic, especially at the beginning. If you have never done this before, aim for five minutes and gradually increase the time. You can officially diary-in this time so that it is reserved and prioritised, even if things come up, which they probably will! Switch off all TVs, radios, computers, phones and games. Maybe use a different room and experiment with lighting, place and position as a cue that you are entering into a special time away with God. Get comfy, but not so comfy that you always end up falling asleep, although God knows that we need that sometimes!

If it becomes increasingly clear that your own home or space provides too many distractions, find somewhere else conducive to quiet and stillness. This may be in a church or cathedral, or walking by a river, borrowing someone's spare room, or seeking out one of the many retreat centres or monasteries which accept visitors nearby. I used to book a morning or afternoon at a local retreat house, manned by nuns! It was so still and there was lots of space to walk or sit. There were nooks and crannies where I could be sure to find a hidden place and the beautiful views helped me somehow to connect with my maker. There are times too when I am led into the presence of God and it gets noisy and messy! In those circumstances as well as with silence, you need to be able to have the space to 'go with it' and I often found just knowing that someone was also in the house, albeit in a different room, would impede my being able to go wherever God took me.

You may find boredom an issue and feel tempted to move on, get up, and get back into normal routine. I have heard it said that going deeper into contemplation with God is like staying seated on a nest of eggs. Hens must get bored too and feel like wandering off, but it's the warmth of their proximity which encourages the chicks to be born. In the same way, holding that silence attunes us more finely to God's voice. Periodically, as a family, we de-clutter our home of belongings we don't use regularly and try not to buy things we don't need. This simplicity helps us to recognise His voice more clearly and helps us to check whether material 'stuff' is getting in the way.

Practising the presence

Once you have found a place of quiet, externally and internally, allow your gaze to be focused on God. Don't worry if lots of other things come into your mind. You may simply want to hand them over, one at a time, inviting God to give back to you at the end of your time with Him what you needed to carry. I used to visualise them as clouds which would then scuttle away, leaving the sky clear blue again. It may take all of your time at first to begin to clear away the clutter in this way, but eventually, you will be left with a deep, lovely, silence in your soul; a peace and a focus and rest in Him. This is where contemplation begins and you can begin to follow and respond to whatever journey He takes you on. He may speak, He may not. This is not the objective of your time together, but just to be together, to become aware of His presence and to be increasingly at rest. This is then the place from which you operate, less stressed out by external circumstances and more in tune with God's perspective, living more and more out of communion with His Spirit.

Breathing is a lovely way to slow down your pace and begin to move with His rhythm. When sitting comfortably, focus on your breathing, notice how fast or slow it is going, and begin to slow it down, holding it a little longer and breathing out fully until you have a new, deeper and fuller natural rhythm. Be aware that God is everywhere and in the air around you; visualise breathing in His presence and breathing out those things which threaten His peace reigning in you. Breathing itself has now become prayer, as wordlessly you are revealing your desire for more of God and yielding to His cleansing and healing in your life.

Once you are used to this practice, you can begin then to respond to God and allow this presence to take you on a journey. You may want to thank Him for His peace and His presence, to tell Him how much you love Him and begin to reveal to Him the depths and desires of your heart.

You have searched me, LORD, and you know me.
(Psalm 139:1, NIV)

I remember for months meditating on Psalm 139 and sensing God finally putting 'you search me and you know me' into context. He encouraged me to visualise lying motionless before him as His eyes scanned me inside. I would practice giving my body to God from my toes to the top of my head; my soul, my mind, my heart, my hands, my spirit and my emotions. All of my being was open to Him, and I knew that even if He were to find some undesirable thoughts or motives deep within, He would deal with my offence and 'lead me in the way everlasting'. It is such a relief to be completely stretched out, soul borne wordlessly before God and without shame.

Soaking

Soaking is another word for the practising of the presence of God. The more time you spend soaking, the more your perspective will change and the more you will begin to soar in Him.

It's important to make yourself comfortable when preparing for a time of soaking with Him. It's probably most comfortable on a bed, or on the floor, with a cushion or pillow for your head. Feeling cold, needing the loo or getting moved on can distract you, so make sure you're not on a stone floor, by a doorway, or in a draught! You can soak in silence, or with music or a teaching audio.

For a time, soaking was when He revealed to me His character. He would show me different perspectives of His goodness, love or forgiveness, or I would get revelation on scripture or begin to journey in the Spirit. These times became so special to me that I would run home from work in order to have as much time with Him as possible. I was completely addicted to His presence. It would induce in me an awareness of the Glory of God, the nearness of His joy and I would feel drunk or incredibly s-l-o-w-e-d down and unable to remember the troubles and burdens I had entered that place with. Bathing in divine love, wallowing in pure goodness, soaking in His sonlight and being consumed by God re-arranges you! The presence is the best medicine I have ever come across (although the side-effects are such that perhaps it should come with a health warning: Don't operate heavy machinery afterwards!)

Ask Him!

When we ask Him to speak, He normally does. I can think of specific occasions where He has responded with silence, but that's either because I've asked him the wrong question or because the silence implies that you are free to carry on in the direction you're going; you can trust Him and when it's time to stop, He'll tell you. His desire for connection with us is greater than ours for connection with Him.

God loves to speak and to show us hidden treasures of His kingdom. He loves to show us around heaven and to tell us truth. So, after you have asked God a question, don't forget to wait, linger and listen to the response. Often I have left things in God's in-tray rather than just hanging around a little longer for Him to answer. Why not practice with asking Him a simple question like, 'What do you think when you look at me?' or, 'What pleases your heart?' or even, 'What shall we do today, Holy Spirit?' This opens up dialogue and soon, communicating with God and honing our discernment about how to move in His love and power will become much more natural.

Taking notice

God wants to speak to us all the time. He doesn't have the same sacred-secular divide as we do, so we shouldn't be surprised if He speaks to us in the supermarket or whilst brushing our teeth as much as when we attend a service or a meeting or settle down to pray. I love to be aware of the reality of His company at the cinema, the play centre and the meal table, sometimes even laying another place setting at the dinner table or pulling up an empty chair next to mine in a coffee shop as a reminder and an invitation.

I recall taking my daughter to an indoor play centre when she was a pre-schooler. I was practicing the presence of God as she was playing and the Tiffany song 'I think we're alone now' came on. There and then, I began to shake and recognise God's invitation to be taken up and fly with him. It was so close and intimate: that pop song became a love song and took me into an ecstatic awareness of union right there in the midst of a busy play centre.

Glitches

As we begin to take notice of things around us, we will develop discernment about when something looks or feels out of place. I call it a 'glitch', and it's a bit like the film 'Hot Fuzz' where the hapless police rookie is being trained on 'special ops' to anticipate crime by detecting when things seem out of context. Learning to take notice of changes to what we normally feel or see is a key to hearing God's voice.

He will also speak through ordinary objects, colours and numbers. Recognising patterns can also be a clue as God will often confirm again and again until we get it! This sort of thing can get a little over-stretched within the prophetic arena, but many things have significance and a message hidden within them. For example, there was a time when I became aware that almost every time I looked at a clock, timer or speedo, the numbers were a repetition of the number 2 and particularly the time 22:22. I knew that one way God often speaks to me is by giving me a clue and then sending me off to research it, so I asked Him if it related to a scripture. I became aware of Isaiah 22:22, which speaks of keys and authority. Having asked God more about this, it led into intercession, a vision and an activation concerning some of the women in our city being released in their authority as 'watch-women'.

> *I will place on his shoulder the key to the house of David; what he opens no one can shut, and what he shuts no one can open.* (Isaiah 22:22, NIV)

When we cease writing off everything as merely a coincidence, we begin to see that some of these incidents, repeated patterns and 'glitches' are clues, like a trail of breadcrumbs to lead us further into the purposes and nuance of God.

Other influences

During this early time of fine-tuning, I recognised a need to stop entertaining anything with my eyes and my mind that was not true, noble, right, pure, lovely, admirable, excellent or praiseworthy.

Finally, brothers and sisters, whatever is true, whatever is noble, whatever is right, whatever is pure, whatever is lovely, whatever is admirable – if anything is excellent or praiseworthy – think about such things. (Philippians 4:8, NIV)

Out went 18-certificate films, thrashy, violent or melancholy music and trashy magazines. For many others, these things are still okay, but not for me. They drain my soul rather than feed it. They made me feel anxious, depressed, envious and thin-spired and they affected my sleep.

But there have been positive influences on my journey too. At first, the supernatural experiences I was having through union with God threw me off-beam as I had no reference for them. In fact, I initially avoided supporting evidence for these phenomena and it was only relatively recently that I discovered books by people like Bill Johnson, John Crowder and the lovely mystics, ecstatics and lovers of yester-year. In these accounts I found agreement with and the language to describe what I was already experiencing in the prayer closet. I had already trawled the Bible and felt assured that experiencing God physically through our senses and encountering Jesus and the heavenly realms were all quite natural and biblical. Also, reading Theresa of Avila, Julian of Norwich and others encouraged me so much. I found their simple ascetic lifestyles and the intensity and passion of their experience with the living God so attractive. So, however God is moving in you, begin to find out about it, research it, read about others who have walked this way before and meet with others who pioneer the stuff now. God may give us other people to encourage us, exchange the baton with and to assure us that we're not losing the plot.

Is that really you, God?

It's great when we start to listen to God and feel like our spiritual senses are opening up and we're becoming 'switched on' to the supernatural realm. But we have to be aware that God's voice is one of many clamouring to be heard. When we get a thought, voice or dream, we need to discern where it is coming from. It could be one of several sources: the Holy Spirit, the enemy, the world, or our own thoughts.

a. The Holy Spirit

Our counsellor, teacher and guide. He leads you into all truth, glorifies Jesus and only speaks the words He hears the Father speaking.

b. The enemy

The father of lies. His words will be temptation, accusation and deception. He does not have access to your thoughts but sees your behaviour and speaks to you in thoughts and through other people. An insult spoken to you may not originate in the person accusing, but through the enemy; intended as an arrow to lodge in our hearts.

c. The world

Can be both good or bad; it influences us through the messages we see or read around us, such as through your environment, people around you, imagery, advertising and the condition of society.

d. Our own thoughts

Our conscious or subconscious "fleshly" or "natural" thinking and methods of processing of issues, actions and things we encounter or see.

To work out the origins of these 'voices', you can ask yourself some simple questions. Which of the above characteristics did the message and the receiving of the message belong to? How did we feel when we 'heard'? God may bring truth and convict us of something, but He will not condemn us, accuse us and make us feel rubbish. If the message brought the latter, we can be fairly sure that the source was satan, the enemy. Does the message line up with the heart of God and with scripture?

God will not contradict Himself! Does it serve us or Him? Our 'flesh' or our own thoughts may often wander inwards and serve to build up our 'old self'. Or, we might be tempted by the enemy that God's words cannot be trusted and that it's okay to go our own way. You can also test what's been said by running it past another Christian.

If you are still not sure, you can ask God to confirm it if it is Him or tell the thought to go away in Jesus' name if it is not. Take your time; only act on something straight away if you think God is telling you to. These questions can help you work out what the sources of these voices are and over time, you will establish wisdom and discernment until identifying God's voice becomes second-nature.

Sometimes God will confirm to me that He was the inspiration behind the message by emotions (feeling a tug on my heart, or crying or laughter), circumstances (names or colours or other things in the room around) or scripture (either in a scheduled daily reading or just by opening up the Bible 'randomly'!) Concordances are great for quickly finding passages on a particular subject, so that you can check whether what you've heard is commensurate with the rest of His words. Having peace about a matter is another indicator, especially if you were feeling anxious before. Learning to recognise a change in emotions or something you detect in the spirit at the time of hearing can give us clues as well.

Obedience and fruit

When we act in obedience as a direct result of our time spent dedicated to God in His service, it will produce fruit. This fruit is character which cannot be stolen or replicated and can only be brought about by the Holy Spirit. If God is showing you something or you are experiencing new levels in Him and the fruit is good, you can rest easy knowing that only good fruit can originate from and be produced by God Himself. The devil has no desire to do this, and we have no power by the flesh or by our own self-efforts to make ourselves holy or fruitful in any way.

Knowing scripture

Becoming familiar and owning scripture for ourselves can really help us get acquainted with God's voice. It might help to use the Bible to look for and read aloud passages which put into words how you are feeling. Jesus is the living word and He doesn't contradict Himself. The Bible and Jesus' words to you should line up. This is a brilliant way of finding out what is true and testing things which are said and are happening around us. As the written word becomes active and alive within us, we learn to believe it no matter how we feel or what our circumstances are. This helps clear out the rubbish and help us to get to know Him. As we grow, scripture will be invaluable in training us to recognise lies and stand in our faith. In the often-quoted description of the armour of God in Ephesians, the only part of the armour which is offensive is the Sword of the Spirit; the word of God, scripture, which is a mighty, sharp and powerful weapon. We can use it and quote truth like Jesus did whilst He was being tempted in the wilderness and it will help us stay on track with our eyes on the prize.

As I was beginning to meditate on scripture and practice the presence of God, I started to re-image scripture. I would put well-known passages into my own words, inhabit the truths and ruminate deeply on them, personalising the words and putting myself into the picture. There is something about writing which enables you to spill out all emotions and thoughts and feelings without shame.

David, the psalmist, poured out his heart, doubts and fears as well as His *selahs* and his raptures. In the garden, after Adam sinned and hid from God, God asked Adam, "Where are you, Adam?" I imagine that our omnipotent, omnipresent, omniscient God was probably fully aware of Adam's location! But He wanted *Adam* to recognise where he was. Letting God in to our brokenness and our pain is difficult at times, especially if we have been brought up to believe that displays of emotion should be avoided, or see certain emotions as 'negative'. We need to learn that God is the safest place, our fortress, our portion, our lover, our shield, the One who fights for us and is slow to anger.

Here is an early example of when I used a re-wording of Proverbs 31 to reveal my heart to God. (Why not give it a go yourself? Submitting our scars and wounds honestly, without masks before God, to heavens love helps us to heal, hear His voice and practice intimacy with Him.)

Proverbs 31: an honest re-working

A wife of noble character - can Gaz find her?

She tries hard to love him, but ends up snappy and nagging him.

She works exhaustedly and with little eagerness.

She gets up whilst it is still dark and provides food for all her family, does a day's work before 9am and is useless for the rest of the day!

She considers the employment pages and circles opportunities whilst God whispers "wait", and "I will provide".

Out of her earnings, she goes to the gym, eats richly and is clothed fashionably.

She sets about her work with regret- surely the grass is greener, and lives for her days off.

She opens her heart to the lost, and gives generously her spare change to the poor.

She extends her arms to the needy, but finds she has little to give, and withdraws.

When it is stormy, she is fearful for her family, and rushes about in the tempest to store and gather provisions.

She is clothed in trendy stuff, but would rather be more generous to others instead, and be clothed in righteousness.

Her husband is respected because people see God in Him.

She teaches children and tries to take God's light with her as she goes.

She speaks too readily, but God gives her wisdom when she stops talking and starts listening.

She watches as her husband manages the affairs of their household and wonders what would happen financially if he were no longer with them.

Her baby arises laughing and loves her. She cannot talk yet, but her Mother knows through her hugs that she goes to her whenever she needs a safe place.

Her husband calls her blessed and he praises her for her faithfulness to them.

She is probably Mrs Average, but longs to be 'the wife of noble character. (2004)

Journalling

Once we have begun to practice His presence and hear Him speak, it can be useful to begin to record these nuggets in a book. I journal and write down everything I sense God saying to me: in dreams, things I notice, things I pray about, words people give me and answers to prayer. These are running records and I normally fill a journal about every three months. In the early days, I didn't think God spoke to me at all and I would write in my journal about once a month if that! In reality, He speaks to us all, all the time. Sometimes, we just don't recognise His voice because we are expecting something really big or loud, or because other things get in the way.

Before I felt I had many words from God for me personally, I began to write Him poetry from my heart. If you are not particularly comfortable with verbal and spontaneous declarations of feelings, intimacy or are particularly introverted, you might find it helpful to write down feelings in letters, prayers or poems.

Here are a few of my early ones: they are a flow of consciousness, an attempt to capture something of this new thing that had burst into my life.

> *My need for you is so great, but if you can make a world, you can meet my need.* (2003)
> *You are the oxygen in the air, the water to the faint, the rest for the weary, the paint in a*

picture, the light in the dark, the signpost to the way out, the essence of life and the beauty in us. As you did for me I will do for you. I will open my heart and give myself to you. You stretched out your arms to include all who see, that you are a gift: completely free. (2004)

Every now and again, I find it really helpful to revisit the journals. I began to realise that when God speaks, it's special. We need to start to take notice and if we are hearing the same thing a few times, that is confirmation of what God is saying. We then need to ask God what to do next and go back to Him frequently and ask Him questions when we see patterns. I love to pull out and gather threads of what God has been saying and see how He has woven His ancient magic into all the situations I had laid before Him. When I feel like I am stuck at a crossroads, my journals help me to retrace, find the 'last thing' I know He said to me and be faithful in that until He speaks with a new direction.

Chapter 4
When God speaks

I mentioned before that at first, I expected God to speak using an audible voice, but I came to realise that He 'speaks' in many different ways.

Pictures

God may speak to us in pictures, particularly if we are visual people, or if we tend to use phrases like, "I see..." to describe cognitive perception. Pictures can be like visions that roll like a film, snapshots that are frozen in time or even just a faint sense imprinted on our spirit deep within us. It is wonderful to recognise that God speaks through our thoughts and not just in the big and dramatic signs in the sky. For me it is often something from left-field that interrupts my normal train of thought: it can be easily missed and sometimes I need the discernment of others to fully pick up on it.

If you have a picture but are unsure of the meaning or interpretation, continue to ask God questions. If you're in a group and someone says something like, "I see a tree," then perhaps a good question to ask God is: "What does the tree represent?" Asking the person to recall extra details, such as what else they can see, or noticing if there is anything unexpected or unusual in the picture, can also help to build a fuller understanding of what God is saying. It will also mature the person's gift and help release freedom and the purposes and blessings of God. Sometimes it can be a lengthy process to get to the bottom of what a picture means, so it might be helpful to ask someone else whom you trust to help.

Jesus taught using culturally-relevant, simple, everyday images and objects to connect with people and reveal His kingdom to them: bread, salt, sheep, wineskins, a bridegroom. Don't feel like a sense or an image that you have is too ordinary, and not grand, holy or weighty enough! He loves to speak through everyday images and isn't constrained by our 'sacred' and 'secular' boxes.

The senses

The senses are a really important way to be aware of the voice or movement of God. As I say, I've never heard Him speak audibly, but have definitely had other senses impacted by Him!

Smell

Some of my friends have an acute sense of smell in the spirit, and God shows them when different evil spirits are present through being aware of an unpleasant smell. Another person can suddenly feel sick or dizzy when there are evil spirits present or when they perceive dark things happening in a particular shop, house, street or environment.

Happily, I have experienced the beautiful fragrance of Jesus and been aware of God's presence through smell. Jesus smells good! I love hearing people attempting to put this incredible fragrance into words: there are lots of similes and metaphors, but all of them fall short. It is, of course, heavenly. You may detect His presence in a room through the waft of his fragrance.

> Tonight during the meeting, I smelt an oily balm, a heavy incense. I had heard about the fragrance of Jesus before and asked God what it was I was smelling. He told me it was the 'salve' in 'salvation'. (April 2008)

Another friend of mine asserts that God has given each of us our own supernatural fragrances. She is attuned to the delight God takes in us and she can tell which of her friends is nearby, or see a person through God's eyes, by recognising and delighting in the supernatural fragrance they carry.

Touch

Our skin is a great detector. It can perceive the slightest change of motion or direction in its surroundings. At times I've been distinctly aware of a wind blowing in the room or around me, which has indicated the manifest movement of God, even though there are no doors or windows open. If you feel very warm it can indicate the fiery presence of God, or His healing.

There have also been a number of times where I have felt the literal weight of God's hand on me: once to propel me out in sharing the gospel, another time to accost and apprehend me, and yet another as an embrace before coming to faith.

Taste

The lips are a very sensitive area of the body and can therefore be good receptors for discernment of the activity of God. They might seem like an unusual means of receiving revelation, but they can resolutely testify to the movement of God. I have sensed a real dryness on my mouth when praying for an area which

God wanted to come and refresh and I have tasted sweet, sticky honey on my lips when God has been calling me to intimacy. Once when I was praying about the body of Christ being fed the pure, undiluted Word of God instead of the grey sludgy porridge it was used to, I could taste the sharpness of cranberries on my lips. The Word tastes 'tangy' and it awakens our senses to the reality of God.

There is such a sweetness to the tasting of Jesus. His food is like pure honey and this sticky goodness manifests in places where His richness and provision are being poured out. References to this sweet-flavoured generosity are plentiful in the Bible. Exodus 16 describes the taste of manna:

The people of Israel called the bread manna. It was white like coriander seed and tasted like wafers made with honey. (Exodus 16:31, NIV)

Psalm 81 describes God satisfying us with honey from the rock:

But you would be fed with the finest of wheat; with honey from the rock I would satisfy you. (Psalm 81:16, NIV)

Our Song of Songs bridegroom addresses His beloved:

> *Your lips drop sweetness as the honeycomb, my bride; milk and honey are under your tongue.* (Song of Solomon 4:11a, NIV)

I have experienced the literal taste of honey on my lips a number of times, in the context of intimate worship, and also in the context of intercession as a sense His forthcoming outpouring.

> *I am in the transition stage of labour for the bride of Christ to come into her fullness. I have the sense of having tasted something deep in my stomach, but it is manifesting as a sweet taste, honeyed stickiness on my lips, which I am desperate for others to taste too.* (April 2013)

Sight

Some people will actually see with their physical eyes and others will sense or just 'know' something in the spiritual realm. We refer to both of these as 'seeing' and both have the same outworking. This is one of the most commonly used sensory receptors for God to speak to us, and as the imagery can be so immediate, those who are 'seers' will often need support to mature their gift. Seers may struggle to find the language to describe what they're experiencing and may appear unconventional as they respond physically to things that are not visible in the natural realm.

God gave me a word to share with someone after a church service once; they told me they knew God was about to speak because they saw me approach as if I were in a thick cloud of incense. Because God had prepared them through the gift of sight to receive a message from Him, and because the word I had shared resonated in their spirit, they felt it was trustworthy.

Hearing

Along with sight, this is probably the most common way we perceive God through our senses. In my experience, it's rare for people to hear the literal voice of God, but when they do, it's pivotal! There have been times when God has allowed me to hear what is going on in the supernatural realm around me: I have heard this referred to as 'spiritual traffic'. I have also heard the subconscious heart-cries of people on the streets who are in trouble or whose lives are messed up. It was so loud that I was convinced it was actually happening, but when I questioned others in the building, no one else could hear it, and it served to increase my heart for the lost.

Joy

Recognising joy, allowing it to bubble up inside and releasing it as God leads, can bring significant shifts in personal circumstances and over whole areas. The joy of the Lord truly *is* your strength. This joy is very necessary, especially when you are carrying the heart of God, to give you the strength to withstand the sometimes protracted impartation for kingdom change and to see the harvest come in. Joy can often be found in the face of a long-standing burden; when you're tempted to despair, it declares freedom, open pasture and a new season.

> *I was being still with God and I had the words 'ridiculous liberty', and I saw myself squealing with laughter, rolling on the floor and kicking my legs, in total delight and total freedom. I was a little appalled at first, as I had never done this before, either in the Spirit or the natural, but knew it was a vision of what was to come; it would bring freedom and release to others.* (January 2011)

Before long, and before I fully understood what was going on, I would find myself in the position of praying for people and instead of using words, I would just laugh and laugh. It seemed to release something new and bring rivers and streams into some very dry longstanding situations. Psalm 2:4 says God does that Himself, and we enter into this position with Him:

> *The One enthroned in heaven laughs; the LORD scoffs at them.* (Psalm 2:4, NIV)

It is because of His victory and His sure outcome that we too can rejoice at the powerless attempts of the enemy to restrain and reduce God's precious kids. The Amplified Version describes it like this: "He Who sits in the heavens laughs; the Lord has them in derision [and in supreme contempt He mocks them]." (Psalm 2:4, AMP)

I have found joy to be very infectious; it's something that people desire for themselves. Recently I was approached by someone who recognised this as a key I had been given and they asked me to pray for the same key to be released for them. I was surprised to hear myself answer, "I can't pray for that for you, but I can pray that God shows you what your keys are, and I can ask for more joy and strength in your life." Being released into being who we are made to be is so important, not coveting other people's gifts or keys. However, when people need strengthening, I will often pray for joy; it's a very real currency and fuel for our ability to stand and overcome.

Dancing

God's sense of humour is wonderful! I took ballet lessons as a child, but wearing a leotard and trying to balance and look graceful were difficult because I was quite overweight, so I lost confidence and gave up before I got to studying *en pointes*. The idea that God leads me to dance is delightful, but funny too! For me, dancing is a sign of His breakthrough and I get completely lost in Him. My whole body is taken up in an expression of overflow towards Him and over my situation (or others' situations). It's not graceful—I don't get a 'ballerina anointing'!—but when it comes over me, I simply must dance wherever I am. Sometimes the dance is thrashy, spiky and thrillingly, punkily victorious; other times it is willowy, spinny and expressive. And afterwards, when the overwhelming desire to dance flows away, I can then stop and rest. Sometimes I try and stop mid-flow, but there's always too much energy pulsing and too much spring in my step and latent heat in my heels. I've learnt not to try and resist the momentum of the movement, but instead to allow my fully-aligned Spirit to teach my body, mind and will to follow its promptings with the same level of liberty.

> *As I was getting dressed in my room, my feet began to tap and then suddenly, like a whoosh of energy had been released, I started to dance! I was turning around and around and crashing into furniture, but resisting the movement was nigh on impossible! It felt like God's finger was on the top of my head, causing me to whirl like a spinning top. I was breathless and exhilarated. I was expressing freedom and total trust in God, withholding nothing from Him and taken up in a physical expression of what my Spirit was experiencing.* (May 2013)

Physical manifestations

When something divine impacts upon something created, it effects and changes it. Perhaps then, we shouldn't be surprised if when this Holy God comes close and visits, touches and inhabits us, it produces a physical reaction in our bodies. We read of diverse and sometimes incredible responses to the nearness of God in the Bible: prophesying, dancing, being dumbstruck, falling as though dead, worshipping, incapacity, fear, trembling and joy to name but a few. Whilst we need to remember that not everyone who encounters God will sense something physically or emotionally dramatic, we *do* know that whenever God genuinely moves, people are impacted deeply and cannot be the same again. Those who have chosen to follow Jesus and have been filled with Him are never without his constant, indwelling presence; that well of life.

But sometimes, God's power falls on us and we feel aware of His presence and glory more strongly. He may be releasing something new or healing deeply, showing us truth or speaking clearly, empowering and refreshing, or refining. Sometimes, He is just demonstrating that He loves us. He doesn't need an excuse to come close and whisper in our ears or pull heaven and earth a little closer! At other times, the presence and power of God rests on us or anoints us in an abiding sense for a purpose known only to Himself.

I have learnt that God always gives us choice. He never controls us or makes us do something we don't want to do. We can draw back from His presence or the things He is showing us and that's okay. There have been occasions where God has been giving me a revelation of something or I have experienced something so intense that I have instinctively withdrawn. For many years, during times of ministry or when people were being prayed for, I made it abundantly clear to God that I did not want to lose control, fall over or have an outburst of emotion. Despite my fears (and at times, disobedience and pride) He was gentle with me and waited. In the end it was the absence of His presence which made me yield and cry out to Him for more of Him at any cost, however it was served up!

I have often experienced God manifesting Himself quite visibly and physically in me, so here are some of the ways that has happened.

Shaking

The first physical manifestation I became aware of as the presence of God hit me was in my legs! Normally it begins with a shaking which increases until my whole body vibrates with the anointing of God. I knew it was God the first time I experienced it, but I had very little evidence to prove it. I was aware that others might notice, so I tried to suppress it by pressing my hands on my knees, but that had the opposite effect. Instead, it intensified and spread through my whole body. I soon learnt that I had a choice: either to look normal, sit still and not make waves; or to enjoy God's presence and care about what He thought rather than be fearful of others' reactions. Fortunately, I quickly made my choice to know Him more, because for some time I'd been crying out to God to feel His presence and see His face. Now that He was answering me, how could I refuse Him?!

I spent time in His presence and just wanted to be face down. I kept mumbling over and over, 'I can't stand in your presence, Lord!' I shook and shook, God was doing something very deep as I had the sense in my spirit agreeing to a commitment to a life of high calling. (August 2006)

Heat and fire

One of God's calling cards for me, and for others when I lay hands on them, is heat. This is God manifesting His presence. Sometimes it can denote healing intended for the other person's body or an outpouring of His tangible love. Fire can come during baptism, the sensation of feeling 'strangely warmed' but from the inside out. Normally when I feel the fire of God, my hands shake and the heat radiates off me and I feel clammy and overheated, a bit like being in a sauna or having a 'hot flush'. It can be quite uncomfortable, but it does mean that others nearby feel the heat, as if they were stood next to a radiator. Once when this happened, the person next to me was baptised in the Holy Spirit and was temporarily unable to stand upright!

Tonight during worship at the meeting I found myself singing out prophetic songs from the bridegroom to the bride, His redeemed. I was aware of feeling very hot and heat coming from my face. I prayed to hear the sounds of heaven, and I heard a trumpet heralding Jesus's entrance. Later I sang a song of ascents as my spirit rose up. (May 2007)

I woke up feeling very fiery, with the desire to see churches set ablaze. It feels like my hands have rocket fuel in them and I am dangerous, as if my eyes are burning with fire. I feel like I may have to shout or run today in church! (June 2012)

Coolness

I love that there are no rules with God; He is not restricted to one extremity of temperature! Feeling

His coolness through your body is so refreshing, like an ice lolly on a scorching day or a cold compress when you are feverish. One woman I know detects the manifest presence of God through coolness in her hands.

> *I was being filled again by the Holy Spirit. During the talk, I felt a cool sensation trickling down from my head downwards like an epidural drip. I felt an immense amount of peace.* (2007)

Electricity

There have been many occasions where I have been aware of God using me as a conduit, like a conductor which completes a circuit. Sometimes I have laid hands on people and they've been healed, or they've felt as if a current or electric shock was going through their body. Once, God showed me that if I took hold of a person's hand, His power would move via that hand through their body, out of their other hand and into the next hand that they were holding, and that's exactly what happened! On another occasion, whilst praying for healing for a friend's neck, I felt electricity flowing and sparking from my hands into her neck.

Kabod

At times, God's presence comes with a heaviness which sometimes results in people being 'slain in the spirit'. This thick, rich impact of the Glory of God is called the '*kabod*'. This isn't like a blanket which presses on you and makes you want to lie down; it's better described as a slowness of response or reaction to external stimuli. When people experience this, it is very hard to physically move them; it seems that the kabod isn't just a spiritual weight, but something that manifests itself in the natural and makes people seem as if they're incredibly heavy.

Sometimes the kabod will come with an awareness of the Holiness or Glory of God, or when you have been worshipping or beholding Him. You may sense Him enter the room and move around. Often in these times I see Him as King, crowned and robed, slowly and deliberately traversing a space, bringing in His wake an abiding pull downwards which is hard to resist physically. It may increasingly occur during the normal rhythm of life; at work, whilst getting ready, shopping, and so on, especially as our sacred-secular boxes are blown up. His weighty Glory overwhelms and interrupts us, reorientating us towards the King and His Kingdom.

Having spent so much time in the presence of God over the weekend, when I went to the evening service that night at home, I felt totally anaesthetised and was too heavy to stand up and sit down again during the worship and prayer. I felt as though I would slide under the chair and it was all I could do to keep upright! I didn't really understand what was happening to me, but a friend exclaimed, 'She's slain in the spirit!' (February 2007)

I was praying with a friend and felt the heaviness of the anointing presence of God, like a blanket, heavy, pressing down. A stillness and awe settled, incapacity, a thick peace, a resting deep within, a gazing, a being. (December 2007)

Ruach

Opposite to the kabod is the transience of God, which feels fizzy or tingly through your body. This airy tickley-ness feels like Champagne bubbles and often comes as a result of receiving the breath, or 'ruach', of God. I've never asked or prayed for this specifically, but the breath of God usually comes when I'm in the Spirit: beholding Him in simple adoration, perhaps already having experienced the kabod; or in times of musical worship. Once the clutter has been cleared and I'm fully focussed on Him and enjoying Him with an open heart, and then I'll notice myself breathing in a different way. The very first time it happened was early on in my discovery of our mystical God and at first, I wondered if I should ask my friend to take me hospital! It feels like being a fish whose gills no longer work: it thinks it's about to expire, but then it discovers it can still breathe, albeit in a new way because it now has a new nose!

My in-breath lasts for ages, as if my lungs have a greater capacity to take God in. My natural way of breathing gives way to something completely new: as I breathe in, I inhale something of God and revelation follows. I'm aware of not needing to breathe out for ages and it feels like I could be sustained for ever on that one breath of life from God. I'm often reminded of the passage in Genesis where God breathed life, the Holy Spirit, into Adam's nostrils. He was no longer just flesh and blood; God had fully birthed Adam's spiritual God-image.

The breath of God fills your lungs spreads throughout your body until your eyes see differently and your whole being is suffused with Him. It seems to take you higher; it gives you expansion and opens up a new realm of revelation. I often feel freedom in my head, as if the top of my head is open and I can just rise up and expand! This lightness can lead to a feeling of drunkenness and fullness in God, or of ascension which propels your spirit and leads you to wander, travel and fly. (I'll expand on this in the chapter on Mystical Union.)

> *I began to inhale the breath of God, and felt like I had a straw in my mouth. I was able to suck it in, like a blowback, for a very long time and once within me, the breath seemed to last for minutes. This came in waves, alternatively with the fear of the Lord and felt like the grace and refreshing necessary to continue to hold the experience of His holiness for what was a very long time. It opened up sight too and I began to see naturally with His eyes more of the things He wanted to reveal and left a lasting deposit of being deeply reordered and realigned.* (March 2013)

The hand of God

The hand of God is not a metaphor: it's a *hand*! I admit it can be a bit of a shock when you first experience the touch of God directly and physically. I haven't experienced His hand many times, but when it has happened, it has been very purposeful and motivating and it has moved me into a new level of obedience and responsibility. Touch can instantly both convey a message or meaning and induce a range of emotions and reactions to the recipient; anyone who has felt the hand of a parent on them knows that.

Once God showed me that we can *literally* be hidden under the shadow of his wing and that passages like Psalm 91 are not just beautiful imagery. There was a time when I was feeling very vulnerable and I was sitting in the bustling cafeteria of the University where my husband worked. I allowed myself to get lost in Him and on the threshold of a new world, I surrendered to His leading. I could feel the softness and strength of the feathery wings which had drawn me close to His chest. I could feel and hear His heart beating. I found myself praying for invisibility because I knew there would be people in that café who would normally come and say hello, but He said to me, "Don't you believe that if you take rest beneath the shadow of my wings, it literally means you are hidden?!" No one saw me or approached me and I knew more of the hand of God that afternoon.

The other times that I have encountered the hand of God have motivated me to lead mission and evangelism in risky areas or with churches for whom mission was not part of their culture. It can feel a bit like 'The Motivator' on the television programme 'Total Wipeout', a huge airborne mallet that would give the contestant a shove if they were taking too long to embark on a challenge! Like a fledgling bird before its debut flight, shall we jump or be pushed?

Awakening

By the grace of God, there are periods when we can suddenly have our eyes opened to the reality and nearness of God and His presence, like a rainbow that suddenly explodes in the sky in front of us. Suddenly, our eyes are open in the supernatural realm like a door that has swung open. The disciples' eyes were suddenly opened on the Emmaus Road and they saw clearly who Jesus was, even though he had been transformed.

I was once given a prophetic word where I was told that like Snow White, I had fallen into a deep sleep. My slumber had lasted ten years but the Prince, the lover of my soul, was coming to kiss me awake. Not only would my natural eyes open, but I would also have the supernatural realm unlocked and visible to me. Sure enough, within a few months, God visited me and I was rescued from simply existing into a fuller, brighter, lighter, bigger reality where the nearness of God was incredibly tangible. I was now able to perceive and interact with this underlying, overarching layer, the Kingdom of God or life in the spirit, which had superseded my limited earthly bricks-and-mortar reality.

> *I am experiencing many new things in God; rendering me unable to do anything but behold Him, pouring out my heart in prayer, exposing lies, feeling God's presence very keenly, hearing sounds which make my soul feel like it's going to burst! This is the ongoing filling, the repeated dipping, the overwhelming of the Spirit of God.* (March 2007)

Unfortunately, many Christians have believed that salvation is our point of conclusion. It's not: salvation is just the beginning! I find myself going through seasons of longing for awakening in the body of Christ. Along with all of creation, I cry out for believers to grasp their inheritance as sons and daughters, to operate under their new identities and move on from our 'first date', which although beautiful and important, is just the beginning of our wonderful journey in eternity. When they awaken to the truth of who He is, who they are, their new positions in Him and all the goodness of relationship which is fully available and in generous supply, they will begin to live and reign out of the metronome of the Kingdom of God. I have a shout inside which I cannot fully articulate but sounds something like, "Come on sons and daughters, ARISE!" We don't need to dance to the rhythm of the media, popular culture or opinion or the rest of the world; our puppet strings have been cut and we are enlivened by and grafted in to the freedom of the rhythm of heaven, in pace with the Father. Only God Himself can produce awakening in individuals, across a nation or in His body as a whole, but we can play our part by yielding to it in ourselves and being willing to pray for it in others.

Overshadowing

I remember being at a New Wine event and Heidi Baker was speaking from Luke's gospel about Mary and the annunciation. We heard that as Mary submitted to God's plan, she was overshadowed by the Holy Spirit and became filled or pregnant with breakthrough, the Messiah Himself. There are times when God overshadows us. We are filled, overwhelmed, undone, fully surrendered and wholly useful to the vision, plans and purposes of God. Being overshadowed in this way can instantly replace all doubt and fear with a heart that says 'yes', whatever the calling and whatever the cost. Cost becomes insignificant as worship takes over, faith explodes in our souls and our eyes are captivated by God.

> *After Heidi Baker released a prayer for overshadowing, I was indeed overcome by God. I was completely surrendered, released into total intimacy and birthing, seeing God's heart and going deeper. I was utterly wrecked and He is in total control. My Spirit was dancing and frolicking like John the Baptist leaping in Elizabeth's womb, and it looked to others as though God was playing with me.* (August 2008)

Power

Sometimes I will get the distinctive sensation that corroborates with the Biblical truth that I am, in fact, royalty! I suddenly begin to walk slowly and with purpose. I have a crown on my head and I feel the power of God pulsing through me. As I walk, I imagine waves parting and people bowing the knee to Jesus on each side. Just the physical act of walking then brings the kingdom to where I place my feet, like Peter's shadow, which fell and brought everything under it into healing and wholeness.

I recall going on a journey with a friend in London. As we arrived at the train station, the reality of our regal nature beamed down on us like a spiritual coronation or knighthood. We both walked in silence, knowing without words that we were both experiencing the same power. It was exciting, like that thrill you get when a huge set of Christmas lights is turned on. You could almost hear the sound of a 'generator in the spirit', there was so much *dunamis* power (God's inherent power for performing miracles) being released. There was a surge of gracefulness, purpose and inevitability; all striving had been removed. We simply needed to walk to release His power where our feet were placed.

> *...and the people all tried to touch him, because power was coming from him and healing them all.* (Luke 6:19, NIV)

> *Yesterday I went into work as normal, but felt overcome by the presence of God and began to attend to Him. I felt like there was too much presence and power within me and that it needed to be siphoned off. I began to release it as I exhaled, and felt like I was blowing life and releasing power. I prayed for whomever I could*

lay hands on at work! I told my prayer partner this morning... she had only just been reading the passage in Luke 6:19, where just the power of God was emanating from Jesus and healing all the people, without Him even laying hands on them! How wonderful that as God trains us in these new ways in the Spirit, He shows us that His son, our model, was already doing them thousands of years ago! (May 2013)

Drunkenness

The first time I ever heard someone talking about drunkenness, I thought they meant on alcohol! Someone who had seen me enjoying the presence of God described me as a 'secret drinker'. He was simply referring to the fact that you can know the presence of God, soak in it and enjoy Him! Being with God in this way, especially as the time becomes more and more protracted, can often result in a feeling like drunkenness, like the disciples in Acts felt when the Holy Spirit was poured out again. It's better than earthly wine because it's free, it feels wonderful and doesn't result in a hangover afterwards! It removes fear, draws you further into God's purposes and leaves you captivated by Him. People who are in love, drunk, captivated, taken up and utterly convinced and enamoured by something or someone will often do extravagant things or act with an out-of-character boldness. All inhibitions and fear of man are removed; your sole concern is Him and His pleasure. You are held by love itself, utterly satisfied and complete, and it literally takes you out of your mind and into the Spirit.

Self gives way to Him alone and He takes you through the gateway into the things of heaven. Being drunk in the Spirit is really fruitful as you begin to manifest what you are beholding. In Acts, we read that after the disciples were filled with the Spirit and behaved in a manner that necessitated the explanation, "They are not drunk as you suppose!" they went out and they were able to preach in all the different languages of the people in the city at that time. Scripture often endorses wine and vineyards and invites us to drink deeply, repeatedly dip or be filled continuously. I often feel drunkenness flooding and replenishing me whilst abiding in His presence, on my own or with others, and especially after leading groups or publicly praying, speaking or worshipping.

Drunkenness and joy are always closely linked in my experience, especially when God is using me in church situations as an offence or an abrasion to reveal the hearts of others to themselves concerning

God or to bring breakthrough to a person or situation. I rarely feel sober when holy laughter bubbles up in me to be released for the kingdom!

Often I have been in a Christian gathering or just going about my daily business and it's felt like I've been the only one enjoying the new wine and hanging out in the wine cellar. At first, it took some getting used to. I would often fight against it or try to 'keep it together' in front of people I thought would disapprove. On occasions, it would even offend me, my fleshly religiosity squirming whilst God enveloped me in heavy, woozy contentment. Twice I have been in different churches, assisting the visiting speaker, and have been so hands-on in the messy, levelling Glory that I have had to be carried out to the car by the church leader!

To be honest, I have moments where I fear what others think or pride rises up in me. Sometimes I long *not* to be a sign and a wonder, a person who looks foolish, but instead to demonstrate the seemingly more 'acceptable' signs and wonders that come with more obvious fruit. There have been many times over the years when I am the only person crashed out on the floor or laughing out loud for minutes on end in a meeting. I've cried out, "Why me?!" but the same answer always comes back (and has been confirmed by others): "Because you are willing."

The litmus test with something new, unknown or unusual is to pray to God and ask him to confirm whether or not it is Him. If it is, I normally yield to it and ask for more. It is a choice; as I have said before, God does not force these things on me. The place I have happily settled in now is this: if God is the originator, I will happily receive and transmit whatever He wants to pour out. Something is being released supernaturally in those moments that I do not fully understand, but my primary delight and reason for existing is to serve my Father faithfully, in obedience and in and out of season, and to enjoy His presence.

As we mature in these things, we need to develop our understanding of what is meant for the private times of intimacy with God and what is for the corporate times when we meet as part of the body. We won't always get it right—I know I often haven't!—but His grace is *so* huge and He will show you how to walk in the fullness of what He has called you to. Sometimes it will be in wide-open pastures and safe communities where anything goes; at other times, out of respect for the people or the context, we may have to temporarily hold back.

Chapter 5
Revelations of God

Revelations of God—who He is and what He looks like—and knowing the mysteries of His heart often will come out of intimacy with Him. As you get to know any person, you will know what pleases them, what makes them smile and what moves them. I decided that I wanted to be the best waiter for God that I could be; not just knowing His heart, but also the nuances, the breaths and the things which are spoken the most deeply when no words are being released at all. The secret place, the garden, the place of deep intimacy is for everyone. It's beyond all limitations; it's where you behold Him face to face. Thanks to Jesus, there is no veil of separation. As we spend time with Him, we will discover more and more secrets, the mystery will be revealed and we will have the honour of seeing Him 'up close and personal'. Heaven is open: look up; come away; rise up; discover more for yourself. This stuff is not just for the prophets of old, rotting away in the annals of time, and neither is it reserved for church leaders or the 'anointed' few. This invitation is for us all, and it's supremely exciting, full of anticipation and expectation.

I will never forget being at Chester Zoo and hearing the unmistakable roar of a male lion. It thundered and carried through the air to the opposite end of the grounds. I was quickened with fear and excitement and we rushed to the big cat enclosure. The sight that greeted us was fascinating: the lion was slowly and deliberately pacing around a female, displaying his power and desire for intimacy. With one determined step after another, he traversed the enclosure and then stopped to look directly at me. He stood majestically, barely three feet from me. Only a thin mesh fence separated us. Time appeared to stand still as we beheld each other. I barely breathed or moved a muscle; my eyes took in his huge paws, his beautiful markings, his rough thick mane, his unswerving eyes, his authority, size and stature, his power and his royal demeanour. After what seemed like an eternity, he turned away and resumed his back-and-forth pacing; I was left speechless, flooded with amazement, fear and delight. That brief encounter with a wild, majestic force of nature was exhilarating. Those around me understood the significance of the moment; it had created a special, magical sense of unity and community.

That moment was made all the more intense because in my imagination, that lion was like C. S. Lewis' Aslan and I was encountering something supernatural of God. Now, if a created and caged animal can have such an overwhelming effect, how much more superlative and outstanding must our beloved Uncreated One, the Lord of Lords, the Father of all Creation be?

I refer to my revelations of God as 'sightings' and even though words are woefully inadequate to capture the magnitude and beauty of the One I love—His face, His heart, His character—I've attempted to record a small number of them here.

The heart of God

To some degree, those who have compassion will sense the heart of God. Getting closer to God often takes us to the edges: He will bring life out our difficult times, take us out of our comfort zones and lead us to be the answers to our own prayers. He is found among the poor, the least and the lost.

God asks us to stop. He will show us, one-by-one, who to be with and what to do. He has taken away all fear, and I have found myself having cups of tea in the home of a local drug dealer, coming up against and removing strongholds, watching and praying at court hearings in a murder case, confronting spirits and having demons manifest at me, tackling injustice, hearing the most difficult confessions and living amongst mental illnesses and other oppression. He is always more than enough.

The Holy Spirit was heavily anointing me during worship. When it came to the end and the start of the talk, I was the only one left standing, still engaging with God. I felt like I was being anointed with oil and it was dripping down. God showed me more of His heart, wanting me to minister to the 'least loveable' and as I said yes, He showed me the extremes of what some of them may be. I was aware that some of them might even be objects of hate. (September 2008)

I went to see Jesus Culture this evening. It was such a powerful night. Before I set off for the evening, I had already seen myself in the spirit laying on the floor at the concert, so by the second song when the presence of God really hit me, I knew not to resist. I felt Jesus so close to me, as if we were lying on the floor together. Around me, people were singing and crying out to Him for His presence, and there He was, already present, tangibly, physically, with me. I was in this place for hours and overwhelmed by God's love, but I sensed strongly that the Father had revealed Himself to me. Somehow, without the paramedic support someone had suggested, I managed to come back down to earth and drive a carload to McDonald's for a late night snack. I felt different and deeply connected to the Father. His heart blazed within me and my eyes felt like lasers, full of love. People couldn't hold my gaze because they said it was like looking at the face of God. As I looked at each person, I felt the Father's love for them and spoke over them. It was overwhelming; it hurt; it felt like smoke was billowing at the back of my eyes and at some points I had to look away from the person or squeeze my eyes shut. Heat was pouring out of my hands and at the site of the stigmata, they burned and power flowed out. Those who moved closer to my hands felt intense heat coming off them. One girl and I connected in the spirit, meeting, chatting and knowing one another as sisters without words; I could see her and I knew her. As I looked at another person, I saw an area from when they were a small child that God wanted to heal emotionally. I was able to speak over people as their heavenly Father and affirm what He saw as He created them. On the way back home, He showed me that no-one is Fatherless; He is Father to all. (October 2013)

To this day, if I feel overwhelmed by the Father heart of God for someone, or feel that burning, blazing look coming from my eyes, I know to ask God whom He wants to reveal more of His love to. I must simply be a connector, like a conductor which God may flow through.

The love of God

The love of God is an unchained, fully released river, which flows quickly and freely. It has no limit. Sometimes His love overwhelms us with its passion and extent. God is constantly demonstrating to us His love and passion for us. There are general clues and personal gifts everywhere, if only we had the eyes and uncluttered lives to see them. For example, the sky with its brushstroke of intense pink; the effortless swooping of a bird on a thermal; the wild and untameable crashing of waves upon a shore; the lingering cuddles of my daughter; drifting off to sleep in a freshly-laundered warm bed; the fragrance of vanilla; belly laughter with friends; my daughter wide-eyed with innocent delight; goose-bumps caused by the beauty of a musical phrase; witnessing a talented actor communicate a universally shared experience; being generous to others; having time to go to the gym; crackling fires and a hot drink; being with others in the midst of His presence and sharing lives in spirit and truth; the ecstasy of knowing Him; His kingdom breaking out; freedom; people with courage standing in the opposite spirit to the prevailing culture; a friend meeting a need that was only voiced to God. All of these gifts have God's calling card for me. They are clues to His love for me because He made me and knows what will delight my soul. What are yours?

The Spirit of God

The Holy Spirit is an enabling, dynamic power, full to overflowing with energy. Moving in the flow of the Holy Spirit is like being plugged in to a huge power supply. He is like dynamite, energy or an explosion, surging and bursting forth. There is no containing or controlling Him. He is creative, colourful and on the move, giving us new ways to worship and experience God and revealing Jesus to us.

The holiness of God

Sometimes, especially in worship, you can get a glimpse of the holiness of God. In these instances it is nearly impossible to remain standing; you may be taken to your knees, face-down or frozen! The holiness of God is not a comfortable, floaty, warm feeling, but abject awe, silence and stillness. His majesty commands it.

> *Tonight's worship gathering was so intense, it was heavenly. I kept hiding my eyes and trying not to move a muscle. God was so big and so close. Holy. I just wept. After this, I had a heightened sense of the Kingdom of God, like I had grafted into my body spiritual antennae! It is now much more real than the world around me.* (August 2008)

The cross

The cross is a powerful and frequent punctuation mark. Coming back to the cross regularly is not dwelling on doom, but resting deeply in what has been completely finished and sorted without question. Jesus is no longer on the cross; He went into the grave, He rose again and He ascended into heaven, where He remains, enthroned and glorified, until He returns to bring all things together in Him. I do not need to feel guilt or shame; instead I thank Him for that place where all my sin was dealt with once and for all. Often I will camp out there if God reveals lies or heals memories. Sometimes the cross is so close that my head can touch the foot of it. In that place, I know the sweet presence of Jesus and am utterly convinced that my business with the Father is complete and that all the things I have brought before Him have already come under the full power of the resurrection.

About five years ago, I was following the Stations of the Cross, as celebrated in many churches at Easter time. I was worshipping on Maundy Thursday and was suddenly aware of such overwhelming love from Daddy God. I was totally convinced that Jesus is who He said He is, He died on the cross and He took all my sins. As I was playing and singing in the Spirit, I saw Jesus on the cross, His face twisted in pain. Behind Him, I saw Daddy God smiling at me with a smile that was so open, warm and inviting, and I knew that was only possible because of Jesus. It conveyed beyond any doubt what I had hitherto only known in my head: *it is finished*. I recorded this experience in a poem called 'Easter Revelation':

Recklessly, I begin the journey;
Haphazard, unfocused, but hungry.
And that hunger leads me on.
Your Spirit comes over me, and
Leads me to confess...
The dove gives a lingering glance.

Passive moves to active.
The search becomes purposed
Approaching the throne room,
A pilgrimage in worship.
Time stands still for this heavenly moment.
As I sing of your grace,
I feel your walls of protection,
And as wild beasts blunder about
I am locked into a tangible peace-
My eyes only on you.
They haven't gone away,
But I won't take my eyes from you,
And the intimacy increases.

Taken up with you, and in you—
And I am convinced in this moment
That Jesus made the way,
For I know the love of the Father.
I am feeling His eyes are on me,

Everything within me sinking into His arms.
A love-exchange which leaves me melting
So close I can hardly dare to breathe
Surely nothing can touch me now...
So warm, so real, so open
Is your invitation to come closer.
Can I really?
Is there any deeper than this?

And then I see the Son
On the cross, his face twisted in pain—
And behind him, You are there,
Smiling at me—no, grinning—a real smile.
As he took my sins, he made the way.

And I know, for the first time
That I am loved by the Father.
I have seen the look in His eyes.
Surely nothing can separate us now.

And here I pitch my tent,
With Him loving, and taking my breath
away.

Rabboni? (Easter 2008)

The blood of Jesus

Another time, God showed me the power of Jesus' blood. He began to speak to me about 'insignificance' and how I believed lies about who I was. As God revealed lots of curses that had been spoken over me, I confessed them and forgave the people who had said those things. In the Spirit, I knelt at the cross and put a stone in a bucket for each curse and hurt. Then I brought those people to the cross; so there was the bucket, the people and me. Then I saw the blood of Jesus fall like a blanket. It covered me, those people and the words they had spoken. (I didn't realise the blood could cover things as well as people.) Then He whisked it away and they were all gone. All that was left was me and Him. I was free!

He also gave me revelation which left me with a permanent illustration of the separation we have from sin. I had come to God, aware of being tempted and circumnavigated by my prowling enemy, the devil. A friend simply walked straight up to me at work and brushed accusation off my arm—he later said that he saw the grip of a claw on my shoulder—and with that release, I began to kneel and pray. I saw Jesus take it all on the cross and descend to hell with it: not just sin, but sickness and sadness and all my stuff, and not just my stuff, but everyone's stuff, and not just now, but the past and the future and for all time. I was rooting for Him, waiting and wondering what would become of Him and how it would be dealt with. I later saw Him shoot up like a rocket out of the grave and it wasn't with Him anymore; it was still in the ground, far away from Him and far away from me! I felt God's love again so strongly after this revelation of grace and truth.

The dominion of God: heaven

Heaven is the realm of the dominion of God and His fullness dwells there. It is a place which can be accessed simply by faith. Begin to read the scriptures concerning heaven and allow yourself to entertain the possibility that this is not simply pictorial language. When people describe being taken up into heaven in the Spirit, they *actually go and visit heaven* and see, hear and experience the things of heaven. Angels live there and there are many rooms and many places for people to be taken to. Worship is always fresh as God is enthroned and heaven-dwellers are always seeing something new of Him and His nature, His beauty, His purity, His holiness, His otherness, His love and His goodness. It never runs out because He never stops being. It is a place of ease and freedom and the pace is different. There is no sickness, crying or pain. The striking thing about heaven is the Lord and the Bible is clear: we, you and I are seated in the heavenly realms with Christ.

So, put aside unbelief if you have never encountered heaven before. Close your eyes if it helps. By faith, allow yourself to become aware of that reality. You are seated. *Can you feel it? You may even be on the throne.* You're in the heavenly realms. *They are all around you. Can you hear them? Can you begin to sense what's going on?* You're with Christ Jesus. *Wow. What is He doing? How does He look at you? What sense do you get from Him? What is He feeling?* As I go into this place through faith, I often see myself in my mind's eye sitting on the throne next to Jesus. It is a place of intimacy and honour and the throne is big: I know this because my legs swing like I'm a child at her new desk on her first day at primary school! Often when I have been praying for someone or a situation, Jesus will say, "This is easy; come up here," and there I am, sat beside Him. Then I will lean forward and gaze over the canopy of heaven: there are no obstructions in front of me and despite the sheer drop, I am not scared. I peer into the earth like a globe, scan in and see the person, city or situation from God's perspective. And then I agree with Him.

Praying this way is so much simpler. It's a surprise and a relief.

The fear of the Lord

Those who access heaven will probably encounter the fear of the Lord. I adore it! It falls like a blanket, brings wisdom and separates those things that are eternal and matter greatly from those that are temporal and immaterial.

I confess that I used to be a little afraid of my father and used to feel deep regret when I had displeased him, even though in reality he's a gentle giant and not at all threatening or scary. It's tempting to imagine that our heavenly Father is like our earthly one, but He isn't. We shouldn't relate our experiences of earthly parents, carers or influencers to the Almighty God: He is totally 'other'. The sense of the word 'fear' actually relates to the awe, reverence and majesty of God. How might you feel in the presence of Queen Elizabeth? But He is the King of Kings and Lord of Lords, and how much do you know it when He comes close and reveals His position! In my experience, there is only one response and that is to *get down*. It is very humbling. It puts everything into perspective in a single moment. To a God like this, your body has no choice but to completely defer in hushed awe, not wanting to move a muscle or avert your gaze until you are absolutely sure that the train of His robe has passed by.

It was only last weekend that I experienced this again. My friend Cassie and I had a goodnight hug and as the fullness in Jesus in each of us met, He suddenly took us into a new level of His glory. That 'quick hug goodnight' turned into hours of being held hostage under the heaviness of His presence.

> *My first recognition was of trying to stay on my feet but the heaviness of His presence incrementally pushing me first to grip onto the banisters, then kneeling, then face down. His holiness was the primary characteristic I was aware of, then a combination of the fire and the river, which came in waves. The fire and the holiness made me weep through my Spirit with involuntary gushes which bubbled up from deep down. The river made me want to giggle. A strange combination, but Him, and the sense of holiness was definitely the most imminent. I felt I was bowing along with the 24 elders and wasn't sure how I would ever get up again as I kept seeing new sides to Him, new and fresh waves of His holiness. This was also a place of revelation*

and birthing. I was like a red carpet, rolled out for Him to traverse. All people could see was Him as I was so low down and He was clearly visible. (March 2013)

I had a great time praying today with Bob about sacred economics, the kingdom-alternative response to the issues we see around us. The fear of the Lord descended, awe-ful and fright-ful. Silence landed. To bow and say nothing was the only response. To obey and surrender without words was imperative and unrushed. I felt like Moses, hidden in the rock. And even as that heaviness lifted, to speak afterwards was in a whisper and faltering, knowing I was lucky to still be alive. I wondered at how people literally lost their senses in biblical stories after encountering the living God and found myself waiting a good half hour after prayer had ended to open my eyes to make sure that Holy fear, the Holy One had passed on. I felt that if I peeked, I would be sure to see one of His eyes and I knew I would be done for! I felt my way to the toilet with my eyes still closed, understanding why the cherubim have so many hands to cover their eyes, in case, in looking up, you caught a glimpse of His glory, another pair of wings could quickly clasp over your eyes. Bob mused that whilst some covered their eyes, others had eyes all over their bodies; eyes being receptacles to His glory. These beings were given over, modified, in order to be receivers of the pure-light glory. (December 2012)

Rooms in heaven

The scripture writers record Jesus speaking of going to His Father's mansion in heaven where there are many rooms. He promises to prepare a place for us. Heaven is expansive; there is enough space for all of us. I have been in several rooms in heaven and I'm aware there are many more to be explored.

The throne room

I was in an experience of thousands of people worshipping together at a conference. It was an incredible atmosphere, and I began to sing in tongues, sing intercession and felt the wind of the Spirit blowing me. The Glory came and I went face down on the floor. I saw our worship rising like incense, a hazy line rising upwards, and I was taken up through a glory shaft. I saw myself twirling and dancing before the throne, and although I could hear the sounds of heaven, there was no one in sight but me. I was dressed in white, dancing in delight for the Lord, around and around, and I saw bits flying off me, and I was totally abandoned to Him. Slowly, and gradually in real time, I fell over sideways from kneeling and stayed there, wholly undone and surrendered. I could hear in the room that the corporate time of worship was coming to an end, but I could also hear heaven's sounds: a cacophony of noise which all harmonised wonderfully. I didn't want to ever come back." (August 2007)

The ballroom

Being in the ballroom dancing with or for God is one of the most intimate and passionate spiritual realities I have experienced. The ballroom feels to me like a really big room with huge ceilings, lots of gold, dark wood and parquet flooring. Every time I go, I am the only one in the room. That is not to say that I am the only person dancing in the ballroom, but I believe I see myself alone because I am aware His eyes are on me; He is captivated by me and I dance freely and without restriction for the audience of One.

I have a recurring image of me dancing in the Spirit, but it is balletic. I am wearing 'pointe' shoes and dancing so gracefully; in gentle pirouettes or skaters' lay backs, with grace, control, ease and proficiency. I go beyond the perimeters of what my physical body is able to do; such is my abandon to God. I have two senses at the same time... That I am a child—free and having fun—and that I am representing the bride of Christ—intimate and romanced. (June 2007)

Jesus is the door. I was in rapture and immediately we were dancing; like a Baroque, mirroring, courtship dance, but when we were separate, it was unbearable and I pulled Him close to me. I just wanted to be held by Him. I felt so small, so covered, so protected. I told Him I wouldn't pull away and that I wanted to go higher. Desire took over and I was very emotional—such rapture and so intimate in the dance. It is overwhelming how close and how beautiful He is. I am undone, and He hasn't even said a word yet...! I am so drunk with bridal union. Keeping it simple and diving into the depths of divine love seems to be the only way! (February 2013)

You can experience the reality of heaven wherever you are and in whatever situation you are in. Once I was taken up whilst on a train:

> *I was focusing on Jesus on the train and felt the invitation to dance with Him. My prayer was, 'Jesus, I want to get so close that I can look into your eyes,' and as we danced closely together, He showed me that as we were intimate in the dance. His fragrance was transferred onto me and I became a carrier, a brazier of Jesus Christ, so that all who see Him are changed. (June 2007)*

Another time, I woke up one morning already drunk in the Spirit. I was holding His hand and we were dancing together on a huge wooden dance floor. It was wonderful; I knew in that moment that I was 100% His and He called me His daughter.

The courtroom

There is a lot of teaching emerging at the moment about interacting with the Courts in heaven. Like courts on earth, you can go there to present a case and bring the accused to trial. God is the judge and the courtroom is in session for you whenever you need to use it. People have seen great mountains move through activation of the Courtroom. Like any other room in heaven, you go there through faith. There is no formula, but I am learning that the more you honour and acknowledge and thank God for what you are imagining or seeing, the more it seems to open up the realm of revelation. Then you can just plainly state the case, why something is unjust, and ask God to judge. Of course, we are not asking God to judge people, but against the enemy; strongholds; injustice; sickness. We can then ask Him to release the opposite—justice, compassion, mission, generosity and so on—so that the church is realigned with His will and His justice.

I went into the courtroom, and before I went in, I began to see it through my peripheral vision as I was already in the Spirit. There were rows and rows of chairs, with beings seated; a full council. God was sitting, enthroned before me. I came humbly but boldly and I knew there was no hurry. They have been waiting for my case and it is very orderly and quiet. I pray, ask forgiveness, receive the blood. The spirit of 'x' is brought to court and I present my case. I look at God. For the first time ever, I can't distinguish between God the Father and Jesus. It is equally both of them. The next thing I know, the spirit of 'x' is lying on the floor in a heap like a discarded residue of gases, dirty, black and thick. God, dressed in white (righteousness) has stood up to absolute silence and is standing, pointing and declaring judgement on the spirit. God is dark, thundering, scowling. His wrath is focussed on the spirit. I have never seen Him like this before, but I know He has my case in hand. I see how terrifying it is to be on the receiving end of God's wrath and judgement; I become aware that I will face Him one day and I am mightily glad of the righteousness that I stand in because of Jesus. Later, I went into the court room again. I was surprised to see myself enter in royal robes, and walking in a bold and stately way. I had come first to repent but had the sense of this being just a formality as God saw me already as righteous. (January 2013)

The strategy or war room

Like many of heaven's rooms, I stumbled upon the strategy room in prayer without previously being aware of its existence. I was seeking God with my prayer partner and so that we could pray in line with heaven, I felt led to bind the eyes and ears of the enemy and our fleshly thinking. We asked for the room to be sealed so that we could hear the mind and voice of God alone. Suddenly, I had the sense that we were in a locked-down, vaulted bunker. It was white and spacious, oval in shape, with rounded walls and a large table in the centre. It felt safe and the atmosphere was of thorough efficiency and decisive victory. It was like being in a vacuum: the silence was monumentally huge, cavernous and deafening, and the enemy could not hear us at all.

God began to show us secrets and strategy. He made us aware of what 'enemy plans' we were opposing and gave us guidance on what to do about them. He debriefed us about the stronghold we had come to seek Him about: how old it was (about 500 years); how it had come into the place it was residing; what it was called; what it looked like; how it manifested. He showed us that we were not able to deal with it at that time, but gave us a vision of how it would be defeated in the future. This revelation showed us that although this stronghold seemed threatening, it did not require a great deal of prayer at that time. As we came out of prayer in the war room, the nerve-centre of His heavenly communications and planning, and back into our natural surroundings, we were struck with awe for God; His command, His certain victory.

The wine cellar

Intoxication comes when you receive the revelation of unbroken 'Romans 8' union with God Himself. We are invited to come and drink richly and deeply without cost, our soul delighting in the richest of fare.

There is a place in the Kingdom of God which looks and feels like a wine cellar. It is lined with huge old wooden barrels and has a big door which can be locked from the outside or the inside. You may work through a number of different types of drinks in the Spirit; each one has a different glass, tastes different and has different effects. God is a very generous host and will see to it that your glass is topped up regularly. Unlike drinking in the natural realm, drinking in the spirit has only positive effects; even if you are a serious imbiber, there is no sickness or hangover. It is pure, deep, full and free... and highly recommended!

> *God is taking me deeper, through deep and deeper yet! He is up high and when I want to come down, He is there also, the anchor! I am*

hemmed in by His love. It's like falling down a rabbit hole; it's crazy deep, more and more lost-ness and found-ness. I am pretty gone yet find myself crying out for more and I am simultaneously totally satisfied. What bliss, how caught up! I knew I was going far out, but this is a tumbling further and further, a secret consummation. I have nothing to say any more about anything. Even if I could speak, I would just point upwards. I am so drunk! Three days straight in the wine cellar. Fine wine, strong spirits, shots, huge barrels, and a lock on the door. Wave after wave... All I can do is put my heavy head down and rest it. I can't sit up straight in a chair, which is tricky. I have been asked several times if I am on medication or drugs and told that I look messed up. This bliss brings utter and total loss of inhibitions and great, deep joy. (March 2013)

Streets of gold

I had been experiencing the sheer bliss and ecstasy of knowing God whilst praying with a friend over Skype for what must have been an hour. We were suddenly aware of the presence of angels in the room, and when we began to thank

God for them and giving Him permission to have His way, He opened up a portal and invited us to come up. I was suddenly in heaven and I was aware that I was walking, tentatively, one step at a time. I was also aware that I was barefoot as the surface felt cold to my feet. In many of my visions and experiences of heaven, I am barefoot, so that didn't surprise me, but the sensation of coolness underfoot did. Seeking some explanation, I looked down slowly—it seemed impossible to do anything quickly or at earth pace here—and I saw that I was walking on streets paved with smooth big stones of gold! It was like the yellow brick road from 'The Wizard of Oz', dancing and sparkling with gold, but it was smooth gold, with the feeling of ocean-smoothed sea glass. The stones were not sharp and there were no definite edges to any of the pieces which made up the glass-gold paving. I began to freak out and weep, aware of the reality that my feet were actually treading on the streets of Gold as cited in the book of Revelation! I couldn't handle it and I sort of sank back into the reality of another place. Hours later as I recalled where I had been, I looked for the passage in Revelation and was freaked out to read this description, true to what I had experienced only earlier that evening...

The great street of the city was of gold, as pure as transparent glass. (Rev 21:21b, NIV)

Heavenly gifts

In recent times there have been reports from all over the world of God pouring out gifts and signs from heaven. It's happening in meetings, on the streets and in the homes of those who are seeking Him. Feathers; jewels; gold dust; manna; all things which are impossible to put an earthly value on, but which simply seem to be gifts from the Father to indicate His proximity and His pleasure in His children. Unexpected changes in the weather can also be part of these indicators, such as rain downpours which are a promise of refreshing, or thunder and lightning which can indicate His majesty. It has been documented that rain has occurred indoors. At a meeting some of our young people attended a number of years ago, the power went out in the tent they were meeting in. When they began to worship and declare the faithfulness of God despite what had happened, the lights and sound were resumed, accompanied by the very strong presence of God. There are signs everywhere, if you have eyes to see!

However, we mustn't seek the signs, but the Lord Himself. Ask to know Him more and by all means tell Him that you want to see things as He sees them, but then simply enjoy him. These gifts are the added decoration, the cherry on top of the cake. Let's keep Jesus the main deal.

> *I was releasing everything to God and had the sense of the sacrifice of my life being transplanted by His purposes and the Holy Spirit was putting something in me. I did not fall even though I felt the heaviness of His presence, but continued to receive more and more from God, with my eyes on Jesus. During prayer, I experienced a feeling like childbirth and people were commenting and looking at the gold dust that had appeared on my hands and arms. I looked at my palms and forearms and there was a fine shimmer of gold all over them, but I kept my eyes on Jesus.*
> (June 2008)

Angels

The first time I was ever aware of angels was when a friend of mine casually told me that he could see my angel. It freaked me out a bit, to be honest! I had previously thought angels were only for Biblical times and these days were much more prevalent in the new age movement. If people talked about having an angel or seeing one, I backed off, thinking they were flaky! However, as I began to learn how to yield more fully to the reality of the presence of God and experience heaven, particularly whilst leading worship, angels helped me to lead people into the presence of God and to join in with heaven's songs.

Before I heard angels or the sounds of heaven with my spiritual ears, I found that I simply began to play them from my Spirit, whilst interacting with heaven and God translating it for me, without my brain involved at all.

> *I was worshipping with a friend and asking God about the sounds of heaven. I began to allow my fingers to travel along the keyboard and play in the Spirit. As I played, each note 'hung' in the air and leant on the next one. My friend, as I played, was describing the sounds of angel voices. We were taken up together.* (July 2007)

Here's a thought I had at the time: does our worship in spirit and truth cause heaven to listen and the angels to gather closer to join in, or does the proximity of the angels cause us to join up with heaven as we then enter into their never-ending praise explosion?

Tonight we heard angels at the worship group practice. We were in free-flow worship, all with the same harmonies and melodies, playing in the Spirit. All of us sensed God say 'stop' at the same time—one person felt a hand on their chest and I couldn't physically play or sing any more for shaking!—and when we stopped, I heard the angels continuing for about twenty seconds afterwards It was awesome! (January 2008)

I sang with some worship leaders from America tonight. At one point, I somehow felt out of sync with what was going on in the room. At first, I assumed I wasn't supposed to be in the worship group that evening, and I knelt down, surrendered to God and was really desperate to listen to Him. Suddenly I became aware of phasing out of the room and into the reality of heaven. I heard angels singing and excited, I stood up and began to sing into the microphone what I heard them singing. Imagine my surprise when at exactly the same time, the guest worship leader, began to sing the same as me but in harmony! We were singing in the Spirit and joining in with the angels. The combined sound was far greater than the capacity of the room that night. (November 2008)

Interactions

I am increasingly aware of the presence of angels, although to this day I have not yet seen one in bodily form. I have sensed them, played with them and known of their presence, direction, increase and activity. Sometimes people bring their angels around with them and when people walk into a room where you are sitting, the presence of their angels can have an effect on you.

Because angels spend their time in the manifest presence of God, they will often bring a whole new stratum of glory with them. This is another way I can detect the entrance and presence of angels. Sometimes I will move in a different way; if my body is inclining, falling or reacting in a certain direction, it is often because there is an angel or angels on the other side of me. There was a time when I was with a friend and my daughter at the local ice cream farm. A new level of glory opened up which was so insane that I was bursting with breakthrough joy: I couldn't eat my ice cream! I knew there were angels but I couldn't see them. My friend responded, as casually as you like:

> *There are two angels, one to your left and one to your right. One of them is writing in a book and the other has a bowl. Every now and again he will pour stuff over you from heaven!*

Some people find feathers around them and attribute it to the prevalence of the angelic; others are aware of colourful or bright gossamer, or lights flickering and dancing around a room. If you have noticed things like these before, it might be the start of an increasing awareness of angels.

The home of angels is heaven. They are sent from heaven by God with assignments to do and people or places to occupy, guard, bless or fight for. People can be assigned angels at different times of their lives if they are going through difficult and dangerous times, walking under a new anointing or starting a new ministry. If you sense or see angels, do honour and welcome them. You can ask God what they are doing and cooperate with them in the plans of God.

Playing

Sometimes I can be playing with angels in the Spirit before I am aware of it physically or mentally. A friend pointed it out to me at work the other day: she said, "Are you connecting with heaven?" and it was because my arms were in the air, swirling around. I was feeling, playing with and interacting with something in the 'thin place' that's all around us and was above my head.

Another time, we had some new friends around for dinner. This was the first time I had ever played with angels before. I was becoming more aware of heaven and beginning to phase out of the conversation. Eventually the wife asked, "What are you doing?!" I answered that I thought I was stroking a cloud. She responded, "Well, I can see that you are playing with angels that are in the room. Your right hand is submerged in the feathers of a large angel's wing, and your left hand is stroking and playing with a small angel on your left."

Playing with angels can lead us deeper into the heavenly realm and release something over people, a room or a whole area. Last year I was at a conference with a friend. It was lunchtime, and we were both too heavily under the influence of God's glory to attend the afternoon session. We remained where we were and before long, we were both playing with angels. I could feel the angels were very big; they had come to release something into the gathering that afternoon. My right hand began to meet with resistance as I was running my fingers through the light feathery wings or cloak of the angel, and I asked my friend to see what she could feel. It's hard to describe, but it's like skidding whilst driving; smoothness gives way to 'bumps' in the atmosphere. As we touched this area with our hands, we found that our hands were cupping something spherical; it was an orb we were 'holding'. This was new to us, but we could feel the buzz of electricity throbbing from it and could see a bright light being emitted. We both felt it right to release this orb and send it to the front of the meeting hall.

By this time, the afternoon session's worship had begun. When we prayed and released it, something suddenly changed in the atmosphere; it brought a real shift, and suddenly the room was filled with the awe and fear of God. The worship group stopped playing; everyone hit the floor and a huge, deafening silence suddenly pervaded. The King of Glory, dressed in His robes and wearing His crown, slowly, deliberately and wordlessly traversed the room. No one moved or said anything for quite some time afterwards. I am glad that God sends his angels to change the atmosphere; God knows we need it! If we ask Him to come, we shouldn't be surprised when He does.

Focus on the One

Even though the angels are beautiful and full of glory, we must be careful not to focus on them and worship them. They are merely signposts to the One who is the most beautiful and glorious. God will lead us further into being able to cooperate with them if we ask Him more.

When God begins to open our eyes to the supernatural realm, He wants us to be ready for what He is going to show us. Each beautiful, pure thing of His has a distorted, counterfeit opposite from the enemy. It is rare that God will open our eyes to the beauty of heaven without also showing us the battles, strongholds or spirits which His angel messengers have come to protect us from. We might be surprised by what God shows us if we ask Him to see more of the spiritual realm.

But we don't need to fear these realities. God already has His victory and the safest place for us is with Him. Nothing dark can stand to be anywhere near His bright, white, piercing, expansive and explosive light. As He kisses us awake, we will have our eyes opened to the reality of the bigger picture, which only serves to reveal more of the majesty of God and reduces all else to naught.

The way in

There is much imagery and language linking the angelic with openings into heaven. Perpetually associated with angels are words such as doorways, thresholds, stairways and portals. We see this in Bible texts as well as in historical and contemporary Christian mystical writings. In Genesis 28, Jacob saw a ladder stretching from earth to heaven with angels ascending and descending on it, and it brought Him into an experience of God where his and his descendants' destiny was released. We should be wary of complicated formulas concerning keys to accessing heaven, especially when they point in directions other than Jesus. Jesus is the doorway, He is the opening, He is the angels' ladder, He is the way to the Father. Knowing Christ unlocks heaven.

We can ask God to teach us more about angels. As we learn, we will sense their presence more frequently, be reassured by God's protection, be aware of the seasons and the times we are living in— times to battle and make war, times to lay down and be restored and strengthened—and grow more proficient in co-working with them on different levels—personal, family, city, nation, and wider—for the glory and purposes of God.

Chapter 6
Mystical union

Christian mysticism is simply communion with God. It is to *know* God rather than to know *about* Him. It's a place where your spirit enjoys harmony with the divine. It is revelling in the truth that we are *in Christ* and that this is a permanent state of being. We cannot 'come out' of it and we never have to try to get 'back into' it. Our state or behaviour cannot effect our position in Christ because His work is finished; the grace-gospel is banked for eternity and *nothing* can separate us from the love of God in Christ Jesus! Contemplation of Him brings connection, oneness, completion and His manifest nearness; there is no parting from Him.

> *Neither height nor depth, nor anything else in all creation, will be able to separate us from the love of God that is in Christ Jesus our Lord.*
> (Romans 8:39, NIV)

God is a mystery who wants to be truly known and He shows us things clearly so that His Glory is put on display and Christ is revealed. I believe we have each been made with the capacity to hold His Glory and display different characteristics of Him to the world.

Creation itself shows this: not content with the one-dimensional colour 'blue', we have royal, kingfisher, sky, navy, teal and periwinkle to marvel at. And then there's us: we are all different and we all display brilliant facets of our creator: tall; short; beautiful; interesting; intelligent; caring; creative; practical; entrepreneurial; simple; teaching; experiencing. A spectrum, an extravagance, a beautiful variety; He clothes and constitutes all His children, whether they know Him yet or not. But in the knowing, there is a revealing, a crowning and an unveiling which bears witness to the work and character of Christ in us, the hope of glory. We have been made for pleasure and the pleasure of relationship.

So there it is, mystical union; the awareness of an unbroken connection with God, the consciousness of being grafted in and in-dwelt by Christ in whom everything is brought to completion. Mystical union, as well as our joy and inheritance, takes us beyond the incapacity of ecstasy and into His purposes where we arise and shine 'for such a time as this'.

The first time I became aware of mystical union with God, it was immediately manifested in a physical sense. It impacted my whole being and came as quite a shock, especially as I was in a meeting full of people!

> *God began to stir up deep emotions and it left me praying, 'Break me, keep me broken,' as I loved the reality of being attached to the Vine. It began to build up, in gushes, the worship inside of me. I felt like I was breathing in Jesus and my lungs were expanded and my breathing getting fuller and fuller. I could hear and feel my heart beat from outside of my body. This took over my entire body, and at times I wondered whether I could take any more.* (March 2006)

Surrender

The Lord will never take us over without permission. We always have a choice, initially to enter into a relationship with God, and at many stages afterwards when He offers a greater depth of freedom or forgiveness. The more we surrender, the easier our 'yes' responses to Him become, until our will is intertwined with His and we become unable to say 'no'. Knowing Him uncovers fathomless riches and the delight of dancing with the trinity.

Come away

God will often invite us to come away from the crowd and into a remote place with Him. I began to recognise this early on in my walk with Him and as I read the gospels, I also saw it modelled in Jesus' life. For Him, it was a place of refreshing after He had been ministering as well as a place of envisioning and discernment as He prepared to hear the Father's voice and make major decisions.

> *The Lord is telling me loud and clear to be still, to come to that secret place, to shelter under the shadow of His wings, to get well acquainted with His voice, to live in the day and not worry about tomorrow.* (June 2008)

I began to obey this request and found such treasure there. Rather than a discipline of silence, it became a joy and I would rush home just to spend time resting and soaking in Him. It didn't matter what time of day or night it was, I just wanted to steal more time with Him. At this point I was unaware of the blessed union we share, so it felt like a quickening you get before an important meeting or a romantic date where you're meeting a person outside of you. However, it became a very important time where I grew in discipline and sensitivity to His voice and where my heart was separated unto Him.

Falling into glory

> I've come up close to You, into the Holy place
> Jesus you're all I seek, until we're face to face.
> I can't go back again, I have to know you more
> Choosing to spend my days at heaven's open door.
>
> More precious to me than the things I can see
> Knowing such liberty, I'm fully satisfied
> Leaving it all behind, eyes focused on the prize,
> Didn't you know I'd be here in my Father's house?!
>
> Heaven now, kingdom come, glory time, angel song
> Access granted, revelation, lover's kisses, activation.
> Heavy presence, grace re-union, love encounter, joy infusion
> Bridal blessing, consummation, bells are ringing, adoration. (May 2011)

Seeing in the Spirit

As our eyes are opened to more of God, we become aware of the dual realities of the Kingdom of God and the realm of darkness. Both exist whether we know about them or not. I found the film 'The Matrix' helpful to illustrate the reality of an unseen (but completely real) world juxtaposed with the natural, seen world that surrounds us. It's like seeing with two pairs of eyes: we see the natural world with our natural eyes and the spiritual world we see in the spirit. To me it can look like there is a blueprint overlaying what I see naturally. For example, whilst I might see someone talking and smiling happily, I can often sense what is really going on, buried underneath. Sometimes I will see demons in people, often through their eyes. I may see something of God being incubated in someone, bubbling up before it is visibly seen. Sometimes we are there to help release these supernatural things into the natural realm. It is the same with the glory, breakthrough, angels, healing and other things of God which are waiting to come forth.

Sometimes we see things that are coming in the future before other people do. This can bring great strength to individuals and movements, but it can be difficult to understand, especially if what we see is so intense and clear that it appears to be immediate. People may misunderstand what we see, or they may need our help to deal with it. Sometimes we stand with them and contend with God vicariously on their behalf.

When we are called to see the future, it is always through the power of the cross, which is the completed work and victory of God. We shouldn't become obsessed by enemy activity; that's what he would want. Simply position your heart in love and humility, remain in community and don't forget to rejoice, praise and worship! If God is showing something to you, He will establish it. There are times when the most profound prayers are simple agreements with God: "Amen," "Yes," "Do it!"

God is showing me He is using me in the process of exposure. He gives me a snapshot when I look at people. His light falls and I see some of what is going on deep down. (July 2007)

He reveals deep and hidden things; He knows what lies in darkness, and light dwells within Him. (Daniel 2:22, NIV)

Remaining in the Spirit

The more we simply rest and enjoy Christ's love, the more we operate out of the spirit of God. Jesus remained in the Spirit; living like He did is a wonderful way to live. It means we no longer segment our life's activities. Prayer is no longer a meeting; worship is no longer a song; presence is no longer just for inside a church building; 'yes' is no longer an answer to ponder. We instinctively know and what pleases the Father and move in it. I will often pray or speak, inspired by the Spirit, and I don't remember what I have just prayed or said. We are possessed by God! It is no longer I who lives, but Christ!

> *I have been crucified with Christ and I no longer live, but Christ lives in me.* (Galatians 2:20, NIV)

Instead of 'switching on and off', or being anointed at certain times to heal, teach, lead, minister or whatever, our lives begin to flow. You cannot have a conversation with someone without it being spiritual, whether you talk about spirituality or not, because you are a spiritual being. Paul makes this clear:

And we all, who with unveiled faces contemplate the Lord's glory, are being transformed into his image with ever-increasing glory, which comes from the Lord, who is the Spirit. (2Corinthians 3:18, NIV)

The veil has been permanently demolished through Christ's life, death, resurrection and ascension; the heavens have been opened once and for all and they cannot be shut again. Hallelujah!

Because we are predominantly spiritual beings, it is possible to see other people as they are in the Spirit. As we operate out of our new identity, we come out of the flesh and into the spirit and our spirit-being grows. In my experience, symptoms of this can include wanting to connect on a spiritual level with people and increasing discernment and access to the spiritual realm. I've even had others witness and describe my Spirit-woman.

God held a mirror to me and I saw straight away a woman warrior from behind. I was barefoot and had long, matted red-brown hair. I was wearing metal breastplates with leather. I had a sword in my right hand and I was fierce and wild. I had the words to shout in my mouth, and had the sense that I was about to shout and advance! I looked like pictures I had seen of Boadicea, the warrior queen who defeated the Roman Empire. (November 2011)

Several women saw my spirit woman tonight! One lady saw her in the form of a really tall beautiful woman, strong. God's glory was shining from me and it made her cry! It made her rethink her desire to see Jesus because she said if she could barely handle seeing my spirit, how would she react to seeing Jesus?! Another said that God showed her intimacy when she looked at me. She saw Mary Magdalene but could smell fireworks really strongly! (March 2012)

I encourage you more and more to allow your spirit-man or woman to rise up so that increasingly you operate from this certainty. Ask God to hold up a mirror and show you your spirit-being and continue to walk in celebration of your unique destiny in Him.

Spiritual traffic

At times we may hear what is occurring in the spiritual realm; a friend of mine explained that this is known as 'spiritual traffic'. This can be confusing;

sometimes it completely contradicts what we see with our eyes. In those moments, God is letting us see what is *really* going on; we need to be open to what He's showing us and try and understand from Him what (if anything) He wants us to do next.

> *I was worshipping at a meeting and began to hear the cries of people on the street outside. I was so surprised and they sounded so loud I assumed they were literal sounds. When I asked my friend, 'Did you hear those heart-wrenching cries?' they replied, 'No.' Then I realised that God had allowed me to hear the hidden cries of a desperate people outside the church. But what do you do when you have heard something like that? They were blood-curdling, pained, almost animalistic. All I can do is give them back to God and ask Him to move. I heard myself repeatedly answering, 'I will hold your people in my heart.'*
> (June 2007)

I recall being in my room at home, worshipping, when I became aware of noises outside. At first they sounded like a new-born baby, but I soon realised they were much louder than any human could make and were too 'other'. The only explanation I could muster with my logical brain was that a wild animal had got trapped. I looked out of my skylight and sensed it was coming from the direction of the student residential area nearby. It was a torturous sound: I didn't know whether to call the police or the zoo!

I asked God what was going on. He said that what I was hearing was not in the natural realm but in the supernatural. I sensed that it was the darkness manifesting and that a battle was being fought. It made me uncomfortable, but having understood what I was encountering, I was able to watch and pray, asking for angels to be released to prevail over the darkness in the area.

This happened during a season where God was filling me with His fire and it was part of God equipping me to understand more about the opposition and showing me that the battle was intensifying. I have not had that experience again since, but I would recognise it if I did.

Dreams and visions

God is speaking to us all the time, whether or not we know Him or are conscious of His voice. The main difference between dreams and visions is that dreams happen whilst we are asleep but in visions, the Spirit communicates with us whilst we are awake.

The differences between a natural dream and one where God is speaking specifically to us are: the latter is clear and sharper; and it will have a distinct message or meaning. To discern which is which, we can use the fact that when God speaks, He will never contradict scripture.

If you have a dream you believe was from God, ask Him for the meaning or interpretation and if there is anything He wants you to do next. There are many instances in the Bible of God speaking to people through dreams, bringing encouragement, protection, prophecy and provision, or to warn against sin. We need to learn to discern whether the dream is speaking about something literal or symbolic and this will help us recognise what we need to do next. If God gives you a dream where something bad happens, this may be forewarning of a literal event, alerting you to pray that this disaster does not take place. As we walk with God and ask Him, He will show us how to grow in these gifts.

Visions can occur during dreams, but they have their own specific characteristics too. People experiencing visions often strongly feel aware of the presence of God and an alertness which comes with the disclosure. Visions can be so sharp and such an all-encompassing experience that the receiver is impacted greatly; they may retain their clarity and sharpness for many years to come. Whilst dreams may need an interpretation, visions are likely to have a clearly defined and readily-apparent revelation.

Personally I have not had much experience of God speaking to me in dreams and open visions, but I do increasingly 'see' things before they actually happen. At times we'll 'see' things play out in the spirit and then take part in activating them in the natural realm later. Often this happens to me when I'm preparing to lead worship. I'll sit at home worshipping but in the spirit I am leading worship in the venue with the people I am going to be with. I'll do a whole set whilst flowing in the spirit and it will show me what songs to use and prepare me for what God wants to do.

Transfiguration

As we become more aware of our union with God and practice His presence, others will take notice. When Jesus takes residence within us, it is He who lives, looks out of our eyes, manifests Himself and moves us to act in the ways of pure love.

When I was involved with singing and leading worship, there were lots of times when people would testify to my face being transformed by His radiance or even manifesting the face of God. One woman said, "When you look at me, it's as if you saw the whole of me, and I can't hide from Him anymore and must address it." (May 2006).

> *During leading worship today, one lady told me afterwards it was so anointed that my face looked like I was radiating with God. Today was transfiguration Sunday!* (February 2007)

Ecstasy, bliss and rapture

Ecstasy is an elevated state of intense feelings which is triggered by deep contemplations of the divine. For me, it began gradually, like a 'phasing-in'. Nowadays I can be taken up into a place instantly as soon as I begin to focus my affection and attention on Christ. In these times, my awareness of unity and oneness with God, people and creation is really acute. I have never taken the man-made type of ecstasy but I am convinced that it's a pale shadow compared to the intensity of the unity with the Most High God. The ecstasy of God is the real deal; it leaves no unpleasant lows or comedowns. Counterfeits can only reproduce a miserly fraction of the supernatural state of rapture which comes freely to those who know and experience the risen Jesus.

When I first experienced this, it came in stages. It began gradually, like flecks of gold woven in and out of my joy, prayer or conversations about the Kingdom and the King. It was like a momentary suspension which would leave me feeling like I was half-in-half-out of the room, the conversation, the relationships or the reality of the world around me. I was aware feeling high, outside of myself, taken up, expanded; like a new world had opened up.

I wrote this poem to try and capture my initial experiences of the ecstasy of God.

In your presence

Oh God, you are everywhere.
There is nowhere to hide.
I am full to capacity
And close enough to touch you.
You are all-enveloping.
Everything within me responding to you.
Beautifully terrifying.
Terrifyingly beautiful.
Purity and holiness.
Coming uncomfortably near.
I try to hide my eyes.
Touch my lips with your coals.
I am overshadowed, tiny.

You are all-encompassing.
I cannot get small enough.
There is no-where to hide.
Exhilaratingly close to
One of pure beauty.
I hardly dare breathe.
I behold the very present,
All-powerful God.
How high can you be?
How low can I go?
Achingly heart-breaking.
Soul-satisfying, totally sufficient.
Oh God, You are God.
Even with my eyes hidden,
I see you.
Let this last forever.
Intimate and overwhelming closeness.
Too intense for words.
Heaven has collided with earth.
Angelic choirs, shimmering harmonies.
The multitudes united with one song.
Surely I will faint any moment.
Almost too much to bear.
My Spirit takes over as
I tremble and gasp and cry out.
You have consumed my vision;

Never the same again.
Just a glimpse of Holy Glory;
Has won this heart again. (2008)

Sometimes I would be taken up into these places in very normal surroundings. I would be aware of delight and extreme love, like my head was above the clouds. One time I was sat in a play centre, drinking a cuppa whilst my five-year-old daughter played, and I heard a loud, atmosphere-slicing, room-silencing, head-turning laugh in the distance. I wondered who it was, only to realise it was me! But I didn't care; I felt numb to and distanced from all else but Him.

God is showing me that deep is calling out to deep. I have an image of a swirling whirlpool and God's hand inviting me to come further and further in. Alice is going deeper and deeper into the rabbit hole; freefalling without a parachute. Out of the deep also came creation. (July 2007)

Only recently, God asked me if I was ready to go another level. I said yes, knowing that really it was a rhetorical question! After that, the very second I began to focus on Him, I would immediately be in ecstasy. At first the enemy accused me, saying that what I was doing was shameful, that this heightened state was too sensual and 'far gone' to be from God. It came like a body blow and left me tempted to not engage with God at all for fear of going into one of these states. I was desperate to know Him more but worried that I was seeking Him for an experience rather than Him for Himself. I came to the realisation that the fruit of these experiences was a deeper devotion to and adoration of God, a hunger for His presence, and a crystal-clarity which brought a new level of discernment and wisdom. None of these things can be inspired by the flesh or the devil, but only by the Spirit of God.

In time I discovered that there are other people who have had similar experiences. I was relieved to discover that a friend of mine also experiences these ecstasies in God. I also read about St Francis who, as well as talking with animals, experienced and wrote prayers of such mystical union and ecstasy that I felt as though I was communing with a contemporary companion as I read his work. Reading about St Francis, Catherine of Sienna, John of the Cross and others, including particularly Julian of Norwich, revealed to me that the path had already been long-trodden! These misunderstood lovers of God are now cheering us on as part of the great cloud of witnesses.

Although it's new to me and largely unspoken of within the church at present, this union is like ancient water or the rarest and most vintage of wines; deep and mystical and still being stirred up and made available to those seekers who linger at the well.

> *I was praying with a friend and saw Him put a pearl necklace on her neck; it was so intimate and tender. He was dressing a bride ready for Himself. We laughed for hours, the glory was so intense. Then waves came, alternately of deep, heavy rest and utter ecstasy. My heart felt like it wanted to burst out of my body and run around for joy, like thousands of popping candy bubbles were bursting inside of me! I was holding my heart, as if to try and contain it. I feel so connected, so close to everyone and everything and so loved-up. I felt He reached in and grabbed hold of my heart. This is a whole other level; totally past it; out to that place of separation where those who want to find Him will seek Him out.* (February 2013)

> *As soon as I began to behold Him, I was being taken up. I felt the ascent; my breathing was rapturous as if I were reacting to a continuous*

and incrementally superlative revelation of something more and more beautiful, magical and indefinably other-worldly. I felt I could surely go no higher. It felt like I was being kissed. It was so intimate and so intense that words fail; I thought I would come out of my body! I don't want to hold back any more, such a contented love-addiction... The Lord is fitting us for heaven, to live with Him in eternity now. And we can take others there too.
(April 2013)

Ecstasis

Taken up, sweet embrace, eye to eye, face to face
You stroke my hair, I am a child, loved by her Dad, full satisfied.

Coming closer, lovers greeting, floating upwards, union-meeting
Tranced out, eyes close, world receding, heaven zone.

Body weakens, soul responds, kingdom language, bridegroom's voice
Weighty place, grace abounds, peace invading sights and sounds.

Drink your fill, intoxicating wine, compelled by love, this bliss is mine
Pure joy, lingering kiss, unending love, ecstasis!
(April 2011)

Trance and ligature

Ligature, or 'liggy', is increased suspension during contemplation and often leads to trance or rapture before the final stage of 'flight'. You gradually lose awareness of the temporal, physical and visible, but it's replaced with a heightened attention to the divine, eternal and unseen.

> *I have been aware all night long that God feels so close, closer than my own skin. I am sitting under such a heaviness of God that all I can do is be. It feels like He's tilted my head up and now I am just gaping at Him, heavy, done, cleaned, reset and recalibrated. I can't see the problems any more; just Him. My heart swoons at His name. Jesus! I am melting deeper and deeper into His love. My eyes were superglued to Him and I struggled to move for a long time.* (January 2013)

The word 'trance' comes from the Latin verb *transir*, which literally means 'to cross over' or 'to passage'.

The Biblical state of trance is instigated by the Holy Spirit and cannot be self-induced. The trance state is a half-consciousness in which the ability to function normally voluntarily is suspended. The person may not know where they are and might lose the ability to speak, walk or engage with the situation around them, but they always have a choice to come out of it.

My first experience of a trance was whilst I was at work on a project. The purpose was to create a sacred space for people to encounter the living God and my role was to release worship in the spirit throughout the evening and early hours. The trance that evening was launched through hours of exposure to sweet 'in spirit and in truth' worship which led to a heavy kabod-inebriation. God invited me to go deep, like a diver. In the end, I couldn't perform my duties that evening because I was so overwhelmed by His intense, wooing call to the transcendent secret garden.

It was different from the get-go. It felt special, anointed; there was flow; I watched someone being led to faith. I sensed my hands were infused with anointing oil and I began to anoint the instrumentalists. I was aware that I was looking at Jesus. Someone prophesied over me,

'Unconventional ways, regeneration.' I was just wrecked, consumed, intoxicated. I couldn't lose sight of His eyes. It felt like I was in a beam and everything in me submitted to Him. I was aware that I was slipping away from earthly consciousness and drawing closer and closer into His eyes. I put my head on the table and was unable to move or speak for hours. He was telling me, 'You have captured my heart, my beloved, my bride,' and everything faded into the background. That time with Him incapacitated me completely. By now it was about 2am and I was finally able to open my eyes... One of the students exclaimed that she could see Jesus in my eyes. This didn't surprise me... you become like what you behold. (January 2011)

Flight

St Theresa of Avila, a sixteenth-century Spanish mystic, began to experience divine spiritual visions which would transcend the pain of her physical illness. She categorised the stages of mystical prayer. The first was "ligature" in which the recipient is taken into a suspended state whereby external stimuli are less distracting. "Mystical union" is the second stage, whereby distractions have completely ceased to intrude on contemplation. The third stage is "ecstasy" (which comes on gradually) or rapture (which impacts suddenly). The final level, the "flight of the soul," takes the raptured individual in an out-of-body experience.

I have been most familiar with ligature, union and ecstasy but I have also known flight at times. Usually I experience flying and soaring in God, but sometimes God instructs me how to release whatever He shows me.

I experienced a quick succession of sensations. First, my hunger began to levitate me off the floor, but from my belly, deep within. Next was the sensation of bright white light behind me and wings, which were mine, unfolding and stretching out. They were very tall and white, strong and feathery; every now and again they touched each other and made a sound like a swan or large bird's wings beating together. Then I began to ascend, accompanied by waves of hunger which seemed to fuel my ability to be airborne. There was lightness, delight and intentionality. At first it felt a little scary, like being on the 'Air' ride at Alton Towers, but soon it became exhilarating and I was rushing! After a while, I began to become aware of earthly things and suddenly I was grounded again. It was amazing.

(February 2013)

Translation and transportation

In his book 'Ladies of Gold', James Maloney distinguishes between rapture (flight) as being caught up in the body, and 'translation' or 'transportation' as being caught up in mind and spirit as well as the body.[3] As yet I've had very little experience of translation or transportation, but I'm hearing more and more stories where the followers of the risen Jesus suddenly finding themselves in a different location. I have also heard people speak of being in two places at the same time, such as someone being at home in bed, but others testifying that they were in a meeting thousands of miles away, speaking, eating and ministering alongside them. What I *have* experienced is imagining a sick person in front of me, praying by faith for healing and laying my hands on them or anointing their head, and finding out later that the person in question was actually healed. I am unsure whether I have travelled in the Spirit and have certainly never physically transported or translated, but if this is something the Lord has for me, I am totally up for it!

I have also heard stories recently about people physically disappearing as they are translated elsewhere; perhaps on earth, in heaven or even through time. What excites me most about this is that it is happening to anonymous, normal, 'unseen' children of God, those men and women who are simply seeking Him, not the obvious, upfront, charismatic ministry people. Only this week, a friend called to tell me I had appeared in her house to minister to her. She had been on my heart a lot and I had been praying for her at my home, but in the spirit, I must have actually gone to her home. These things are happening increasingly.

Only last week, a friend asked me to pray for his mother who had a leg infection and was unable to go out. They live at the other end of the country, so it seemed natural to go to her, by faith, reach out my hand and pray for her, believing that in the Spirit she was right in front of me. When I prayed, my right hand shook heavily under the healing anointing of God; I had a tangible sense that she was sitting right in front of me and that I was kneeling with my hands placed over her hands where the pain was. I sensed it was significant that only my right hand was shaking. I worked out that it would be over her left leg. I also engaged in some warfare, finding that I was suddenly in a flow of tongues and feeling that I was getting cross at the enemy. Afterwards, I texted my friend to tell him I had been praying and asked where the pain was. To my surprise, he reported that the pain was all in her left side. I realised, in some way that I believe but can't make logical sense of, that I had been to her home and prayed for her leg!

It may be that believers have engaged in translocation and not realised. How often do we assume that something is a dream when actually it is translocation? The more I have engaged with God and stayed in the Spirit, the more I haven't known whether my eyes are open or shut! Either way, I still see the same things and sometimes the only way to tell the difference is to touch my eyelids to see if they're closed or not and whether what I'm seeing is natural or spiritual. I encourage you to be constantly aware of engaging with the Father and to move around the earth freely to do adventurous exploits and intervene in the lives of others.

Connections in the spirit

You can ask for God to show you connections in the spirit. I have heard this described as 'sending out pings' to other people in the spirit to see if something is returned. Sometimes, this connection is obvious at first sight. This has happened to me on a few occasions, even before we have spoken. Typically it feels like I know this other person as if they were my sister or very close friend, or that I already know them inside out. The manifestation of His presence may confirm this to me. It may take a little longer until you talk and then the common vision, passion, heart or connection may become obvious. Sometimes you may walk alongside that person for a length of time, obediently and patiently, until it becomes clear why. Sometimes it is for encouragement when either or both of you feel like you are journeying alone in something hidden and new. Other times, it is that the other person is a missing piece in the jigsaw puzzle you have been waiting for in order to see a vision fulfilled.

Sometimes, a third party will recognise this kingdom pairing before you do! About four years ago, a speaker visiting our workplace took my hand and placed it on the hand of another member of staff. In front of everyone, he declared a new season of collaboration and purpose in our friendship together. It was emotional at the time and both of us knew it was a true and accurate word. We began to meet together, pray and dream, particularly about pioneering mission. This particular collaboration resulted in me supporting my friend to pioneer a fresh expression of church called 'Night Church' which existed to provide a safe place in the city centre, bathed in the presence of God, for people to drop in during Saturday evening and into the early hours of Sunday morning. This volatile night-time city-centre melting pot was not a place that Christians generally ventured into before that. Night Church still runs today and has opened up opportunities for other groups to see God moving in power, particularly amongst those on the edge.

Stigmata

Stigmata are the wounds which were inflicted upon Jesus as He bore the separation of the world from the Father as propitiation, our scapegoat. Lashings ripped his skin apart on his body, nails securing Him to the cross were driven through his hands and his feet, the crown of thorns was pushed down onto his temples and a spear was thrust into His side. We know from scripture that although Jesus was resurrected and ascended, defeating all separation and sin on behalf of creation, His renewed physical body still retains these marks; the only man-made trace we can witness in heaven.

Somehow, God seems to have allowed saints throughout history to share in the experience of His sufferings, to bear compassionately in intercession these same wounds like an echo. Stigmata can be visible—other people witness bleeding palms, wrists, sides or temples—but also invisible, where the saint feels the physical, spiritual and emotional pain but without any visible signs.

This is not to say that the work on the cross was somehow incomplete so that we need to act as propitiation ourselves; Jesus Himself announced it was *utterly* finished and complete, with nothing to be added. However, I believe that He allows us to feel the heart of the Father and His longing to be reunited in full relationship with humankind and creation. It is no surprise, then, that the stigmata are most keenly and strongly endured by the saints at times of greater spiritual darkness, including when the church becomes too readily tainted by the world and exerts wrongful power and authority. In recent centuries, the gift of stigmata has been most commonly bestowed upon unordained and anonymous women, and the current increase in this phenomenon brings me hope in an era where God's daughters continue to experience inequality within the body of Christ.

Paul's words in Philippians 3:10-11 give us a more complete picture than we often bear in the body at this time.

> *I want to know Christ—yes, to know the power of his resurrection and participation in his sufferings, becoming like him in his death, and so, somehow, attaining to the resurrection from the dead.* (Philippians 3:10–11, NIV)

Yes, we want to operate in the power of His resurrection; yes, we want His gifts, His goodies, and the overcoming, joyful life. But I fear that if we deny sharing in his sufferings and renounce the very real problem of the world's pain, we limit our own capacity to 'know Christ'. To know Christ is all my desire, both sides of the coin. I pray my 'yes' resounds as joyfully when sharing in His sufferings is required as when the reality of the resurrection, transformation, power and blessing appear in and around me.

My experience of invisible stigmata is incredibly fresh, although intensity of compassion and the cost of travail, which are part of an unseen communion with and longing for God, have been part of my 'knowing Christ' for a long time. In the context of deep prayer, I have experienced the pain of the nail wounds manifest itself in my flesh, and it wasn't until the second time it happened that I had revelation of what it was!

The first time, I was lying on my side on a sofa with my feet overlapping, praying with a friend. As she and I were worshipping and committing to following Christ whatever the cost, I felt a pain going up through the soles of both feet. It wasn't the sharp pain I sometimes experience with a word of knowledge, but a throbbing, drawing, smarting pain. A few days later, the same thing happened, but in my hands and with greater intensity. It hasn't surprised me to discover that other women have been experiencing similar things for the first time in their lives. These are normal, unordained women—a mum and charity worker; a hairdresser—but they have a burning passion for Jesus and have laid their lives down for Him. If you'll excuse the pun, it seems that something is afoot amongst the renegade army of beautiful, surrendered Gethsemane lives!

I was praying and began to get a strange and new sensation in my palms and rubbed them together, slightly twisting them slowly as I did. The sensation increased and it felt really

uncomfortable. I noticed I began to press down and rub my opposite thumb on opposite palm and alternate hands, and as I did so, I recognised this was where the nail marks were on Jesus' hands. I had the sense of 'sharing in His sufferings'. It intensified and I found myself attempting to 'shake it out', but it didn't work! It felt like a burning, wringing or boring in the lower part of my palms and lasted at least fifteen minutes. Although the physical pain was uncomfortable, it was the spiritual longing which was the more intense, and almost took my breath away.
(May 2013)

We know from John 21 that the Bible does not contain an exhaustive inventory of all the stories of the miraculous and supernatural experiences which occurred during Jesus' and the disciples' ministry. We can only assume that many more happened than are documented, and perhaps with even greater creativity and variety. Jesus Himself said that we would do more than Him. Whilst I am still waiting for the dead to be raised, to see angels with my physical eyes or for bi-location or translation, I am open to the fact that the things the Bible testifies to may only be a starting point. I am open to suggestion that this redemptive hermeneutic, this overarching story of relationship with God Himself, may not only give us a plumb line, but also a springboard to the greater things that Jesus spoke of.

Chapter 7
Following the cloud

I wanted to share some things which I have found helpful in continuing to walk with Jesus—the unchanging One—through change. I have called this chapter 'Following the cloud' because although it is tempting to camp out and stick with the level of revelation we have been shown, God asks us to keep walking with Him, to know His voice and remain faithful.

Seasons

It is important to recognise that God often works with us through a rhythm of seasons, and walking lightly in each season without clinging on too tightly helps us to move on and not find transitioning too traumatic. Thinking in terms of seasons is encouraging because it tells us that if we are experiencing difficult times, they are not going to last forever, even if the season feels long and arduous.

Also, don't be afraid of preparation; sometimes it can feel like God is refining and reordering us, and we will be waiting forever to see the things have been waiting for. The longer the preparation, the more character is borne in you, and the more fruitful your life will become. For Moses, it was 80 years, and for Jesus (even Jesus!) it was 30 years for just three years of "ministry".

Refiner's fire

Refining is a season, long or short, when God isolates and works deep within us. He searches us and separates us from things that are harmful or no longer fit. These seasons are often to prepare us for the next stage in our lives. These times can feel lonely and painful, and if we are not careful, we can fail to discern that the source is God. It is tempting to pray away these situations, believing them to be opposition or attack from the enemy, when in fact they are opportunities for God's rescue through preparation and merciful internal surgery.

Often we will go through a number of seasons of refining. It would be wonderful if this happened once and once only, but we continue to have free will and I am grateful that I don't have to live with the consequences of my rebellion. A friend once said to me, "The problem with being a living sacrifice is that you can keep crawling off the altar!" Only a Father who loves us deeply would redeem our circumstances. As He deals with those things which no longer bring life, we can be assured that the pruning will make way for beautiful flourishing and fruitfulness in the next season.

> *God showed me whilst I was gardening today that as I pruned back those branches which had life in the past but were now overflowing into space where they didn't belong, He was doing some difficult and painful cutting off and pruning of the areas of my life which are now dead, which threaten to overcrowd the new signs of life. It was a messy, dirty job, but I prayed that God would get to the roots, to the main 'feeder' branches. It was all very fresh, especially hearing the deep cutting noise of the secateurs. There are also signs of new life; today is the first day of spring, which is encouraging. I have seen the first butterfly of the year today. Hope!* (March 1997)

I believe that God wants us to burn for Him, to be passionate and yielded to His refining. If we allow His fire to have its way, we'll become a furnace or brazier which people can gather around to experience His warmth and light. A candle can either sit on the mantelpiece inert, or it can be lit; then it gives light and warmth in dark and cold places. It's painful to be burned, but it produces a fruit of light and life.

I have learned that the centre of the flame is the safest place to be. You go through the yellowy-orange flame and are purified and that is painful. But if you keep going and don't retreat, you get to the white-hot centre where no other fire or trouble can harm you. I think this is why Daniel and his friends were not harmed in the den of lions; they had already known the refiner's fire and were devoted to Him. They were already in the centre of the flame when they entered the fiery furnace and the lions' den.

The Holy Spirit was moving up and down my body as I lay down during worship group practice. I was praying for a refining, and I felt my body leaving the floor. I had an image of him shaking off more dross, and as I lay there, felt that He had picked up my feet and was rattling me gently from side to side whilst things were flying and shaking off me. (July 2007)

I know that God is doing more refining. I see that the new is outgrowing the old, like wineskins, and He has given me two images to help me understand what is happening to me. The first is a magician doing an illusion underneath a black cloth and then suddenly producing a bunch of flowers. The second is being in the operating theatre having a C-section, not being able to see what is going on, but feeling something deep within and a baby being produced. In both pictures; I am very passive and not in control. I can see something new is being made but I cannot speed up the process. (October 2007)

During refining times, it is good to be totally transparent with God about our feelings, struggles and questions. Reading the Psalms gave me so much strength during these times.

...The LORD has sought out a man after his own heart and appointed him ruler of his people...
(1 Samuel 13:14)

David, a man after God's own heart, expressed freely what might appear to be a very volatile range of emotions towards God. When reading the Psalms I noticed that a pattern would often emerge, whereby a bout of emotion is addressed to God followed by a 'selah' moment. This word actually appears in the text of some Psalms and it's a pause where the psalmist turns his gaze towards God and appears to have a change of heart. Truth rules, hope floods in, deep worship flows, grace and perspective are revealed and the psalmist is strengthened in his resolve to trust God in His goodness and faithfulness.

How do we connect with God in these times of refining? The familiar practices and ways of devotion may not be adequate spirit-and-truth responses any more. Often silence is all that's needed. Sometimes other people's prayers or worship might voice what's on your heart. It's encouraging to connect with others who have a fresh awareness of the mercies of God—I refer to them as 'radiators'—and it's sensible to ask God to protect you from those who will drain you of what little energy you have left—the 'nay-sayers' and 'Job's comforters'.

Sometimes we will see God refining a group of people or a nation. I believe we have been experiencing some of this sifting and shaking in the UK and the Western world for some time now. They might be intensely unsettling times where the foundations of our society, which is not built on

Christ, seem to be being rocked. This might manifest itself in the church as well as in the world. We must not panic about or wrongly diagnose these things, or presume that they're attack or the opposition of the enemy. Our focus should be on the Lord rather than the problems.

The cave

Last year, God took me to a spiritual place where I had never been before. It's a place where the Spirit of God leads you away from the crowd and into the protection and scrutiny of Himself alone, a search for that which is authentic, honest, real and genuine. It's a place that's 'without'; it's without the awareness of the manifest and tangible presence of God, a place where no human can keep you company, a place without comfort, explanation, timeframe or map. It feels narrow and isolated and the temptation is to return to community, busy-ness and meetings full of human warmth and support. I call it the 'cave'.

In the cave, a new longing arose in my soul for space, silence and simply being. Words were unnecessary as all my thoughts and the motives of my heart were as though they were being amplified to God on a loudspeaker. I felt the path I was walking become narrower, the journey more intense, as God revealed the hidden inclinations and tiniest deviations of my heart. As I heard them—like I was standing outside myself—I felt ashamed, 'done for', but being faithful to Him alone suddenly became of even more importance. He called me to be set apart and gave me a longing for holiness as well as a heightened awareness of my weakness and sin. I had to learn another level of trust; it was like a forger's rock where my faith was really hammered out and strengthened. A scripture that describes trust in these terms that brought me much hope is in Jeremiah:

> But blessed is the one who trusts in the LORD, whose confidence is in him. They will be like a tree planted by the water that sends out its roots by the stream. It does not fear when heat comes; its leaves are always green. It has no worries in a year of drought and never fails to bear fruit. (Jeremiah 17:7–8, NIV)

Although the cave is a spiritual place, it is lived as a daily reality, so it has knock-on effects on your mental state, emotions and physical being. As a very definite extrovert, I found myself exhibiting new introverted patterns of behaviour. People close to me found my complete change of behaviour and personality quite worrying and confusing at first, thinking that I was 'shutting down'; I had to listen to friends tell me I was depressed. I also had to deal with the slur that I was being 'religious' (in the pharisaic sense) because I appeared to be focussing on fasting and wilderness-wandering rather than feasting and freedom-celebrating.

God showed me that He was changing me from a caterpillar into a butterfly. I had naïvely thought that butterflies are just caterpillars that grow wings. As I researched the lifecycle of a butterfly, I realised in pin-sharp detail the enormity of the refining stages He was taking me through. In this process, the caterpillar goes into its chrysalis, totally dies and gets deconstructed, like goo, in order to be a butterfly. I had nothing left, I was hemmed in; I felt nomadic, exiled and homeless, and I was totally and utterly messed up. Jesus Himself went through this process of producing life through dying to self (see John's account of Gethsemane in John 12).

Getting to grips with my new temporary home, the cave, was important to me because it helped me feel as though I was in some way surrendering to God's plan. Defining and embracing my new surroundings was essential in walking in obedience to God. I had utter peace that the journey was of God and that actually, the cave was God Himself. As I engaged with the cave, I could actually sense the shape and depth of the cavernous structure by touching the curve of the walls. I perceived the sparseness of the environment. I began to recognise it as a gift; a place of refuge; a place without lots of external stimuli; a place of being, trusting and waiting. No arrows could reach me in the cave; I felt hidden. I came to enjoy this refuge, this place of stripping away. The cave is essential: it's where the Lord cements His message deep within the prophet, like a seed, which is later released.

One day, weeks later, I woke up with the sense that it was moving day! When I asked God why it was time to leave—it had become home to me by then—God said to me, "The cave can also become an idol," and I found myself being led out to stand at the mouth of the cave, waiting and watching for further instructions.

I suddenly began to dance this morning in the bathroom! I had the feeling of being escorted out of the cave, to the next place of presence, to follow the cloud. All my expenses have been paid! There is nothing to pack and the next place has

already been prepared for me! When you follow God in this way, you can travel light!
(October 2012)

The pitch-darkness of the cave is all-encompassing; when you emerge from it, you really have to adjust your senses. I didn't hear specifically from God in the cave, so I had a sort of culture shock and had to rediscover my senses of hearing and sight, but my discernment had been heightened, so when my senses were rediscovered, they were much sharper. Concerning departure, I sensed that it is important not to leave the cave too soon, but neither should you stay too long; it is a place to leave your grave clothes behind in.

As I emerged from the cave, I realised that it had borne in me a very strong message. I identified a lot with the prophet Ezekiel whose message became part of Him.

> *Then he said to me, "Son of man, eat this scroll I am giving you and fill your stomach with it." So I ate it, and it tasted as sweet as honey in my mouth.* (Ezekiel 3:3, NIV)

I found myself with a new perspective and a new message burning inside me concerning the Body of Christ, but in my home city I wasn't recognised as an authoritative figure or a public speaker with a platform. I found this very unyielding, like David's armour, until I began to look into cave dwellers and prophets in the scriptures. Many of those who have gone before have also endured this refining. Jonah's message was so uncomfortable that he ran away; his cave was a whale! Elijah and David experienced the cave. Ezekiel spent over a year lying on his side in order to represent his people in repentance before God. John was brought up in the wilderness with a calling to prepare the way for Jesus with a message of repentance. Jesus Himself endured the wilderness and the tomb.

When I emerged from the cave, I was totally different. I entered into a season of great freedom, authority, alignment, destiny and seeing new ways for things to be done. The cave birthed a message deep within me; a clarion call to the church. It felt like the Father was reminding the bride of her marriage vows. He was asking the bride to be ready and hang on, not to jump paths, not to settle and not to sell out, but to stay faithful and to see the things we have patiently waited for come to pass.

The dark night of the soul

Symptoms of the dark night of the soul include acute loneliness and isolation, aching frustration and spiritual depression. (Mercifully, it only lasts for a season!) Whilst in this cloud, seeing is impossible and it's as if God is 'on mute'. It can be very confusing. For me it often results in disturbed sleep—like having jet-lag—and in the daytime I feel detached from what's going on. All non-essential, non-kingdom concerns slip away and I feel I have nothing to add to earthly conversation.

The lessons learned in the cave can help, although the dark night feels more like drifting in space than being hemmed-in in the cave. Our questions give way to deep rest and waiting in God with tunnel vision, which brings conviction that Jesus is our only hope. This is a time of transition. Once the cloud has passed—which in the *kairos* timing of God can happen quite suddenly—we realise our ego or 'false self' has met its demise and our soul encounters greater levels of union.

I am in limbo, transition, a holding-pen, having left one place behind, but am not yet released into the next. Sometimes I feel weak, a woman crunched over in pains of childbirth; and at other

179

times, frighteningly strong, with the latent wild potential of a volcano within. I'm like the Hulk about to change or the Doctor mid-regeneration. Occasionally I literally and physically feel God's embrace, reassuring me, but otherwise that is all I feel or know; so I wait... (February 2014)

The desert

The desert is another place of refining; an uncomfortable season where you can feel dry, exposed and drawn apart. Of course, it is important to discern the difference between a place where the Holy Spirit has drawn you for goodness, exposure, healing and preparation, and a place of lowness and despair that the world or the enemy has drawn you into. Sometimes we can accept the arrows of the enemy believing them to be God's voice; at other times, the temptation is to pull ourselves out of a place God Himself has drawn us into for our growth and protection. Although it's uncomfortable being drawn into the secret place, God's work is characterised by hope; when it's the enemy, there is fear, loneliness, confusion, despair and an unyielding feeling that it'll last forever.

Reading David's Psalms has really helped me in desert times. I had to learn that it's okay to tell Him everything: all your feelings and thoughts; not just the 'good and acceptable' parts of yourself, but the whole lot. In these times, we can help ourselves by resting and trusting in God's promises, keeping our eyes on Him and giving Him thanks. This is faith to the max: thanking God and trusting Him when many would say, "Where is your God?"

1 Samuel 30 speaks of a time in David's life when he feels utterly deserted and threatened by his own kinsmen. He has already undergone difficult times, and now he experiences further pain, isolation and danger.

> *David was greatly distressed because the men were talking of stoning him; each one was bitter in spirit because of his sons and daughters. But David found strength in the LORD his God.*
> (1 Samuel 30:6, NIV)

I have no idea how I would have reacted if I had suffered the torments, threats and disappointments that David went through, but he encouraged and built himself up in God. He placed his trust in God to help him, continued to praise Him and meditated on Him as his source of strength.

So, what does that look like for you? How do you strengthen yourself in the Lord? I asked God once, made a list and then tried to make sure I did some of those things.

> *I have been drawn by God into the desert. This is a weak, broken time. But a real hunger for Him is developing, and God is strongly giving me the desire to become 'contrite'.* (April 2003)

I found that in these times, I need to purposely separate myself from external stimuli and comfort other than Him, surrender all my problems to Him, ensure that I'm meditating on truth, practice His presence, live simply and rest a lot. Engaging in simple, uncluttered activities really helps me; such as spending time with my cat; doing craft; soaking in the bath; gardening and reading children's stories (last time I read through David Walliams' books—they were great!).

It was in the desert that I learned to turn away from false comforts. In particular, I gave up alcohol, which had been a problem in earlier life. Nowadays I drink in moderation—out of freedom–but those years without drinking allowed God to reign more in my life. We should also remember that desert times, because they affect us so profoundly, have an impact on those close to us, particularly our spouse if we are married. Seeing someone you love suffer is very difficult; it requires a deep trust of God if we're not to be crushed by the situation. We cannot fix, heal, solve or restore others; only God can do this.

> *I am learning about fruitfulness in the valley; not to seek only the mountaintop experiences. The valley is a place of peace, water and growth. I am asking God if I must be here, to make me a Lily of the Valley, wanting to be a tenant in God and not merely a visitor. It's like I saw myself standing up with my coat still on, and He asked me, 'Are you staying?'* (July 2007)

Monasticism and the cell

Times of refining are often marked by a stripping down and a withdrawal from worldly complications, distractions and persuasions, away from crowds and coffee shops and even the good things of the world. Instead your holistic self is allowed to express its deep and basic needs, such as simple food, warmth, stillness and silence, revealing what really matters; the kernel, the heart of everything. God may seem to have little to say—sometimes the silence is deafening—but His steadfastness and vast presence is very real. I find myself unable to engage with people's debates, game-playing and power battles, but instead retreat and try to allow the Spirit to be free. Just being, being aware of God and resting are all that's required.

Consumerism—filling that gap—is endemic in our society and it's a tragedy when the antidote has already been delivered and is ready to be received for free. The water, the stream of life, the body; the bread of life, the propitiation, the blood of Christ; they never run out and are being poured out for those who will simply receive.

The cell is a colony of heaven, a 'thin place' or holy space, the presence of God in a room. The monastic rhythm is breathing in (intimacy) and breathing out (mission) and embraces worship, simplicity and hospitality. As well as a refining, it can be a tremendously rich blessing.

We have a sense of being called again as a family to adventure, to a radically different life, to fully abandon the flattery and externally- based world approval and embrace simplicity and become holy fools. We have been editing our belongings. There is such an explosion in me to reject, kick away, push back against the crap, become like

John or Noah. This is hidden in our hearts yet has an outward out working. Consumerism is making me sick! We are no longer able to distinguish between 'need' and 'want'. It is a challenge but we hear it; to live forever simply. Simple lives of love, simply and only Jesus, simple so that we are never too cluttered in our minds or too encumbered with our possessions to respond to the call of God or the cry of man...
(December 2012)

It feels like God is narrowing the path. I am finding the 'ins and outs' of family life and being with friends like an assault on my senses. It seems to me that everyone is talking at the same time, it is rushed, frenetic, busy and squeezed; such is the depth of silence and solitude I have recently found in Him. We have begun to make small, intentional choices to reshape our lives which reflect simply God's love. This is a new way: life; deep community; missional; loving. I sensed this is a training ground for what is to come. If He can train us blind, in the dark, then when He shows us the new way, the new places will be instinctive for us, as if we have already been there for some time. In the meantime, God provides us a way to wait; silently, listening, discerning, drawing on Him. Like Paul, would we say, 'I am resolved to know nothing but Christ, and Him crucified.' (January 2013)

For I resolved to know nothing while I was with you except Jesus Christ and him crucified.
(1 Corinthians 2:2, NIV)

Separation from false comforts

As Job well knew, in times of refining and testing there are often false comforts and false comforters which would give us something to cling to other than the Lord. I have heard it said, "You can't be delivered from your friends, only your enemies," meaning that it's difficult to be separated from enemies of our souls if we have made friends with them. For many Christians, sin cycles, eating disorders, addictions, behaviours and thought patterns are so familiar that the thought of being free from them is actually scary. Without 'X', what will be left? Who am I without 'Y'?

I controlled food for so long that it was like a comfort blanket to me. I hated and wanted to be free from it, yet somehow I thought I would be poorer, bereft, half a person without it. Sometimes a season of refining is so that we'll come to a place where we are willing to be free of these false comforts and familiar spirits. The addictive behaviour, the controlling nature, the inability to relax; these surface behaviours are never the problem. Once we have let go of our personification of and connection with these things, God can go deeper, bringing release and freedom and leading us into our true identity and destiny.

Burnout

Two years ago, I was approaching burnout. I had simply been running too hard in my own strength and had neglected the Lord of the work. I had forgotten His acceptance and His rest and was striving so hard to do His work and ministry that I had abandoned the One thing.

I had to have some time off work. This was probably the scariest time of my life because without my work, my identity was totally obscured and I was left with a gaping hole. I felt like I had nothing left and it caused me to wobble dangerously. I realise now that it was vital for God to expose my inner emptiness; He spent a while chucking out a load of old rubbish that I had accumulated like a secret hoarder. This was such a raw, vulnerable time. I saw my situation with fresh eyes, but I was powerless and too exhausted to change anything. It felt like being laid out on an operating theatre table. I would often feel out of control, the smallest task would overwhelm me, and I would find myself weeping without knowing why.

Once God had cleared away all the clutter, He began to re-order and re-furnish the metaphorical house—me—with those things I needed as foundational. I clearly remember the first time that I experienced peace again; it had been so long since I had entertained peace that at first I thought it was numbness! God gave me His peace, presence and then grace... Whoosh, wow! His grace was so immense and so overwhelming. God wasn't standing with His hands on His hips, frowning and tutting; He was loving me, wave after wave. He didn't mention my indiscretion and my wandering eye; instead I met with multiple barrages of prodigal, pure, liquid, open-armed, incapacitating love. He had *already* totally restored Himself to me and me to Him.

I want to encourage anyone who recognises in themselves a drive to succeed, a struggle to stop and rest, or a lack of deep, life-giving connection with God and others. Maybe it is time to get off the merry-go-round, pause and relent and position yourself for a barrage of grace and realignment. God's intervention just before burnout saved my life, and He is in the business of doing this for others.

I realised how long it had been since I had just worshipped. I began to feel His love come and melt me. I felt waves of His love and waves of my love for Him. I was caught up in the middle of that swell, that swirl, that love mash-up. The first thing He is putting back is worship; true love. I feel His majesty coming near; I hide my face. I am lying as if sunbathing and being rocked gently backwards and forwards, like on a beach and undulating with the tide; these are the new unforced rhythms of grace. Next, peace came into the house; connection without striving, guiltless rest, deep down inside and in the perimeter, all around. I feel His grace and favour and I simply kneel, because I receive even though I don't deserve it. (April 2012)

I wrote this poem shortly afterwards:

When I was young, I thought I knew the right way I would grow,
Simply plant a seed, add water and sun, and it would just be so.

Now I learn, as I cling to the vine, that The Lord
must prune the shoots,
We work in vain, unless we let Him deep into the
roots.

What brings me hope, despite the pain and the
slowness of His pace,
Is the promise that we will be instantly changed
when we see Him face to face.

Obedience

There is so much blessing which comes from obedience. Not a blind, slavish, law-full, guilty or proud obedience, but a surrendered, yielded 'yes', which is emitted from deep within us, whether we are suffering the desert places or enjoying the mountain-tops. The major blessing comes from simply being His child and doing His will, but sometimes a simple act of obedience turns the key that unlocks a roomful of blessing. We can mistakenly think that God rewards like-for-like, e.g. if we give money to someone, our reward will be financial. But He knows how to bless and give gifts to us as individuals; obedience unlocks such a blessing.

Restoration

Thankfully, there are also times where God leads us into restoration, often after intense seasons of refining. This is such a wonderful gift: it resets our bodies, minds and spirits and brings rest and refreshment. We cannot give to others what we don't have ourselves.

I don't want to exist in or write and sing about yesterday's stories. It seems that quite often, people's most precious memories are from when they last really sensed God's love and power in and around them, decades earlier. This makes me feel sad: union is constant and forever, every moment is precious and an invitation to drink and celebrate unbroken connection with Him. The best is now, and the best is also yet to come.

If you haven't felt aware of God's love, peace, rest, comfort, equipping and patching up, then stop a while. Invite Him in, allow Him to meet you, attend to and minister to you deeply. Stop being strong and able, slow down, stop, be; wait for His presence. Allow other people's prayers to speak for and over you; allow anointed worship to flow over you as you receive. Take a break; go somewhere remote, beautiful and restful. Connect with nature and notice the little beautiful things again. Accept weakness.

Surrender and yield. Become a 'being' again. You may notice you are able to breathe again. You cease to take yourself quite so seriously; you notice peace flooding in; you let go of judgement and offence; you can feel and see Jesus close and clearly; you recognise beauty in small and insignificant things. You don't feel responsible for everything; you don't get stressed over everything; you become less demanding of others for perfection; you are able to delegate and release to others rather than doing everything yourself. You are now in the grace-place!

River

The river is a wonderful place, a place of blessing, flow and refreshment, where you experience the abundance of God. His blessing is extravagant, superlative, overflowing, lavish, unmeasured and embarrassingly generous.

> *Bring the whole tithe into the storehouse, that there may be food in my house. Test me in this," says the LORD Almighty, "and see if I will not throw open the floodgates of heaven and pour out so much blessing that there will not be room enough to store it.* (Malachi 3:10, NIV)

Once, a friend and I recognised it was the season to rest. In the Spirit, which became our surrender and reality, we were both lying on stretchers by a river. We each knew the other was there with us, but we didn't say a word to each other. We were attended to by angels. They fed us, soothed us and sat with us. I could reach out and dip my hand in the river's waters and allow their coolness and refreshing to tickle my fingers and bring me life. We were mandated to rest, to be, and to be waited on by heaven. It was a beautiful, precious, grace-filled time. We kept reading Psalm 23 and knew it as a daily reality: God's initiation and invitation; the stillness and the healing power of God in the natural world all around us; the safety, rescue and protection; the provision, plenty and overflow. This season lasted for weeks and we both sensed strength coming back into our bodies as we were able to sit up, stroll, soak and play by and in the river. This brought bursts of ridiculous, childlike liberty and joy.

I will never forget my time by the river. I encourage you not to resist if God lays you down for a season. He knows how vital to your soul this heavenly convalescence, this divine treatment is.

My heart was overwhelmed and I went to my piano to worship him spontaneously. As I sang, He scooped me up and took me to the river. He laid me down gently, took some water from the river and washed me. He told me I was free to lie by it, jump up, splash, soak, bathe, jump, dance, paddle or dip my fingers in. It didn't matter—I was free and He was restoring me. I became overwhelmed by His goodness and cried and sang. It felt like I was pouring out oil and wetting His feet with my tears. I was surprised to see how He looked at me. He loved it and wasn't rushing me or pushing me away. Others were embarrassed and encouraged Him to end this two-way display of intimacy. He said, 'No, let her; this is pure worship and it pleases my heart.'
(May 2012)

River and fire

And just when you think you have it sussed, God likes to mix things up a little. There have been times when He allows you to go through the fire and the river at the same time! If you experience this, just ride it out and enjoy it. He knows what He is doing and it is deep. He won't necessarily take you out of the fire but

He's providing simultaneous refreshment! It is the river which keeps you going through the fire.

> *I was enjoying God's intense presence during the evening service tonight. I was shaky, overwhelmed and ecstatic and couldn't do anything but just sit and be. I am hidden in Christ.* (June 2007)

Chapter 8
Prayer, intercession and other callings

Prayer is simply connection with God. For a long time we have put it into a 'spiritual' box and limited it to that which happens when we bow our heads or say, "Hands together and eyes closed," or speak out loud or in tongues. This is dangerous because it leads people to think that prayer is somehow holy, that you need someone ordained, special or gifted to pray on your behalf, you need to be in a church or sanctified place, your life needs to be sorted, you need to be less 'messed up', or you need to use long and religious words, which means that they can't do it. God has made us for relationship with Him and as we live that out, our very lives become prayer. As we begin to still ourselves before Him, contemplate Him and cultivate intimacy, we will sense His presence keenly and enjoy union with Him.

Prayer can take many forms, including wordlessness, shouting and being angry, a surrendered heart, a difficult decision made out of obedience, inviting God into a walk or a stroll, giving and sharing generously with others, or simply letting go of something.

The simplicity and effectiveness of prayer is modelled in the Lord's Prayer: "Your kingdom come, your will be done, on earth as it is in heaven." How simple is that? Prayer does not serve our agendas, so there's no more getting frustrated with God because He didn't do what we asked for or expected. By faith, the Bible says we are seated in the heavenly realms. So, simply check out what's going on in heaven and that's our blueprint for earth.

As I described in chapter 5, sometimes I will be in the spirit and sitting on the throne with Jesus. It's a big throne, my feet dangle over the edge like a schoolgirl's and together we look down from heaven. Prayer becomes such a simple thing: we just agree with heaven! As we wait on God and listen to Him, we begin to pray different prayers than we might have done beforehand. There is peace—loads of it—and a realisation that it is finished. Sometimes your Spirit-led prayers will surprise you; many times I have been surprised by what I hear myself speaking aloud. But His thoughts are not ours and His ways are not ours.

Please know also that God hears every prayer and every cry of our heart. He is not dispassionate or far-away; He does not have favourites or play roulette with His answers. Every prayer is significant and makes a difference, like a hammer blow to a wall. A wise woman once told me that we do not know which of our prayers will be the blow that demolishes the wall, but each one makes a difference.

Pray as you can

Because I was struggling to find my own life's natural rhythm, I once bought a book on prayer in the hope that I might discover the ideal prayer model, the quick and easy "Seven Steps to Improve Your Prayer Life" formula. The first sentence took my breath away: *Pray as you can.* It was simple, refreshing and it blew apart my preconceptions about prayer. (I never read the rest of the book—that sentence was all that I needed.)

After that, prayer became a joy and truly 'in spirit (from the depths of your nature) and in truth (genuine)'. I no longer felt obliged to set my alarm clock really early, or to work up prayer until I was praying an hour or two a day. It became a flow and a delight; a constant awareness and acknowledgement of His presence. Sometimes He woke me early but I discovered I knew in the spirit how to pray. Afterwards I would either immediately fall back into a deep and peaceful sleep or be supernaturally sustained throughout the day without being exhausted. Sometimes I fasted, sometimes I shut myself away to pray, sometimes I prayed for hours—although it might be more accurate to say that I simply lost track of time because I was so immersed in communion with God!—but in all cases, the self-effort, the self-flagellation and the constantly striving to 'do better' were gone.

Sometimes doing something practical can help with prayer. I have found that some people, particularly men, can struggle with the established church's expressions of worship and prayer because they're too feminine or passive. Doing something practical or demonstrative can often feel more real. One friend of mine loves to run. She hears God speaking when she pounds the streets in her trainers. For another, the 'way in' is through soaking and listening to worship. An old colleague of mine used to bring art equipment to our times of prayer and worship. As she allowed her hand be an expression of the overflow of a two-way relationship, she would produce installations that were a blessing and a challenge to the body of Christ as well as being her personal response to God. My husband likes to get away on retreat to pray. One guy likes to book times in his diary to go and have a walk and a pub meal so that he can eat and chat with Jesus. Another friend loves to use visualisations. At every mealtime he will 'see' himself walking on the beach with Jesus and allow himself to go on journeys where they hang out together.

So, you have permission to be! Quietly or loudly, with your whole body or not, using words or in silence, dancing or being still, indoors or outdoors, with liturgy or freestyle, with others or alone, for hours or sending quick arrows up, kinaesthetically or centred, kneeling or sitting. Just pray as you can. And as you do so, allow God to show you your rich identity as a 'son' and heir. Live in that rather than out of lack and striving to be better. Then you will know who you are and what feeds your soul. Prayer, worship, mission and life decisions will flow with ease. You were envisioned before time and created at the right time. You have a purpose and are completely accepted and loved. There are no 'shoulds', 'oughts' or 'can'ts'; run from those things and towards the inner food that will light you up internally.

Prayer and introversion

Many prayer or fellowship meetings centre on those who take the floor and speak the most (or the most loudly). In these circumstances, introverts will often feel insignificant, hold back and struggle to participate, even though they may have heard God speaking clearly and have really valuable insights to bring. We discovered that for some introverts, the prospect of having to say something out loud was quite intimidating. Some people were really helped by being encouraged to write things down; this way they were able to express what was inside far more readily and it meant they could fully participate without being overlooked. Sometimes, those written prayers were read out loud. There were even times when once pen hit paper, such a gushing flow of consciousness would tumble out that these introverts found they had a huge amount to say. Beginning with silence and punctuating times of prayer with quiet, or using a guided mediation, can bring that much-needed open space in community for introverts.

Intercession

Intercession is a call by God to pray about something specific. It can either be something you pray for once or something you carry in prayer for a lifetime. God may want you to pray about a person, a situation, an issue, a street, a city, a nation or beyond. Often they will be situations that require breakthrough or change and an intercessor is someone who is willing to 'stand in the gap' as an intermediary, or temporarily take on some of the feelings and consequences of that situation in their own body and spirit. Of course, it is Jesus who is the true intermediary and He has already carried everything Himself on that cross. But for reasons best known to Himself, sometimes He will ask His people to join together with Him and intercede on behalf of others.

In my experience, it is often the curve-ball of compassion that begins the gift of intercession; not going-for-it prayer, pacing around, binding and releasing or loosening of tongues. I would often hide myself away during small prayer meetings, amidst a room littered with seasoned intercessors who were crafting their words and praying with great authority, and there I would be, kneeling on the floor and weeping, trying not to draw any attention to myself!

It feels strange at first to hold these intercessory assignments close to your heart. Your own situation may be good, with your life ticking along smoothly, your emotions stable and your relationship with God secure, but simultaneously you feel desperation, sadness or frustration; your wrestle is very real but difficult for others to understand. The intercessor, the person 'hosting' the heart and purposes of God, needs to understand this tension if they are not to be overwhelmed by it. The Holy Spirit has shown me progressively how to walk with Him in this: you need to know who your friends are; when and if to share; when to encourage yourself back into community and when to retreat; when to continue walking and when to stop and release everything to Him; how to pray; the safe places to pray; and how to remain connected and built up in Him.

Breakthrough

There are times when opposition seems overwhelming and multiple things come at you relentlessly. When this happens, the main thing is just to cling on until the ride is over! These times can be so intense and long lasting that it is easy to forget how to stand firm in the promises of God. It's important to have people around you who know your situation and can pray according to God's will. God will often turn the persecution we are subjected to by the enemy into blessing, into a springboard or stepping stone to greater levels of glory and intimacy.

There are times when I feel in my body a representation of the spiritual atmosphere around me. It's as though pressure has built up inside me; I feel tense, heavy and warped, and I need to bear it faithfully until it bursts. Often after it releases, in the natural realm I can see the blessings of God, a new level of His presence, healing, breakthrough and an openness which had not been there before. This feels different to labouring and birthing in God (mentioned later) because often breakthrough will come out of the blue, without a prior sense of 'carrying' or 'labouring' a vision of God. Breakthrough can be on a personal level—where there's a sudden change in the state of your inner being—for someone else, or over a geographical area.

Only yesterday, breakthrough came to me in this way. After a period of weeks of illness and the resurgence of an unpleasant stronghold coming against us as a family, lack of sleep, household things breaking and lost assignments, I was starting to feel pretty beaten up. I was easily overwhelmed by the problems around me and, for a number of days, had struggled to be aware of the closeness of God. The persistence and nature of the opposition was predictable and almost laughable! But yesterday I woke with the sense that breakthrough was in the air. I had decided to keep my focus on Jesus rather than on the situation and began to listen to worship music. Then, out of nowhere, I suddenly found myself dancing whilst I was getting dressed! It's as if you're suddenly full of energy and pent-up heat; there's a bounce in your legs, you're inexplicably dancing and it's hard to stop. It's difficult to resist the tide of this supernatural energy! Later... I was aware of the strong desire to worship, praise with my whole being, sing in tongues and express the freedom of the growing manifestation of the presence of God in my physical body. I sensed the increasing glory of God; waves of joy swept over me and I heard myself bursting into laughter. I felt the sweet intoxication of new wine again; my awareness of heaven's reality increased as earth diminished. Something broke yesterday... God declares, 'Enough!' and in a matter of minutes, I am in an altogether different place. My spirit knows how to respond, rise up and burst out of those chains. Since then, whenever I turn my attention and affection towards Him, I am caught up in ecstasy again, focused, rapt by Him and His closeness and beauty and perfection. Breakthrough has come! (March 2013)

It's also good to take rest and look to Jesus until breakthrough comes. When you rest and meditate on truth, your spirit is lifted and bursts out of its bounds, meeting God in the air and propelling you higher in Him. Often God will bring breakthrough through worship, dance or joy. The last time this happened, I was at an evening gathering where a prophetess was visiting. From the outset, the Holy Spirit was welcomed and I began to laugh. I was the only person in the room laughing. Not a polite little chuckle, but a spiritual deep laughter which rippled out from me, for minutes on end; I was rolling around in my chair laughing. The visiting speaker began to prophesy that in this next season for the church, the birthing would be in joy and I was a sign of what God was about to do. For the whole of the evening, I would laugh whenever I saw someone to whom God wanted to bring breakthrough! It was as if my laughter was a peal of bells ringing in a new season for people; He was bringing breakthrough powerfully, spiritually and inexplicably through joy, the anointing that breaks the yoke.

Labour and birthing

As Mary was trusted by God to carry something precious, God entrusts us with people, issues and areas to hold and give birth to spiritually, often after we have demonstrated to Him that we can be faithful in intercession for the smaller things. I don't believe that travailing, labouring and birthing prayer is something God asks of everyone, but it's a call for some who will respond. Travailing intercession is being allowed to stand in the gap for others and it comes from intimacy with God. We associate closely with the struggles of others in the private chamber that God has given us. As we feel the struggle of the situation and emit wordless prayers, we represent that situation before God until His compassion breaks that sin, heaviness and pain and the intense intercession ceases. Great peace and joy usually follows.

The Bible is littered with birthing imagery, even birthing in the spirit. Isaiah 42 really encourages me:

> *For a long time I have kept silent, I have been quiet and held myself back. But now, like a woman in childbirth, I cry out, I gasp and pant.* (Isaiah 42:14, NIV)

Birthing is when God plants a spiritual seed inside you and it grows until it becomes 'full term' and can be safely delivered. The seed can be a vision or breakthrough, and it can be individual, corporate or geographical. As God conceives this seed deep within you, you may have to hold it alone, in the secret place. This might be for protection—so the seed cannot be stolen or destroyed—or because of His *kairos* timing. As you carry this spiritual assignment, it will probably feel very real; you may even have the long-term vision to see what it'll look like when it's released and what the effects will be. But what's plain to you might appear foolishness to others, so it's imperative to hear God's wisdom on the time to release it.

God showed me in a time of prayer that a mother becomes a mother the moment she conceives and begins to carry the baby, whereas a father becomes a father when the baby is born. Mary was alone and quiet when the angel spoke to her about the destiny of her precious baby. Once the baby was born, Joseph had the authority, named the baby and fathered him. I have seen this principle played out many times when carrying something of God in prayer. I have learnt to be careful whom I share it with and when, and I need to be generous and forgiving of others when they don't see it immediately. Once those other people see the thing of God birthed and established, they are far more likely to be on board, but in the meantime, we need to rest in God and keep our hearts soft, because it can be many years from the conception of a vision to its birth. We need to be yielded to God as we carry and birth this spiritual baby because it does not belong to us. We are merely surrogates, wombs for the purposes of God, and we have no right to assert authority or to hold onto the baby once it is born. We may never even get to see with our natural eyes the effect of this long-awaited miracle of God, but our delight is in serving Him and it is a privilege to be chosen as a safe vessel, a hand-maiden (or the male equivalent!) for a new manifestation of the reality of God.

Each time I experience spiritual pregnancy and birthing, I am astounded at how it manifests itself in my physical body. It's so like how my real pregnancy was. Recalling my own daughter's birth and researching others' has helped me to understand the various stages of this deep prayer process and how to take care of myself holistically during it. Here is a description of a cycle of labour and birthing (or partial breakthrough) in the spirit:

I am carrying a longing which manifests as a drawing-down sensation from deep within my belly. When it's released, it's wordless. I have actual contractions which look like my stomach is jumping, and as labour intensifies, the contractions increase, peak and decrease again. Last week I was actually beginning to waddle and feel very full in my pregnancy in the spirit. I have found myself out of breath whilst doing the simplest and least strenuous of jobs, panting, doubling over and have even woken up early in the morning rocking with actual contractions. My husband, who had never seen this before, put his hand on my stomach and saw and felt the 'spiritual kicks' from the inside out! I have been crying out to God; exactly what for I don't quite know; but the longing takes over, the desperation to see the baby born, for release and breakthrough in the body of Christ, so that Christians ('little Christs') become fully alive, glorifying God and being released to 'go and sew' wherever they are. Increasingly I am aware of having very little space in the natural and of feeling alienated, closing myself off, easily irritated, and finding my husband's soothing and comforting suddenly irritating and distracting, as

I did during active labour all those years ago with our daughter. I do not perceive God particularly close, but I have gained a focus and a tunnel vision. I am bearing down and getting through. I have frequently found myself crying, tears squeezing from my eyes, whilst rocking in prayer. This has been going on for ages now, and it feels as if my life as I have known it has been laid aside and dedicated to this cause of prayer. I don't particularly want to be around people as this consumption and intensity is hard to bear. I haven't got the energy to explain it and all my focus is required at present. It feels like such a longing and a wrestling at times. I am asking the questions internally: 'How long?! Will I ever see it? Where is the place for this thing?' (And sometimes, half laughing at myself before God, 'What is to become of me?!'). Only this morning, it was so intense that I knew breakthrough would have to come; there was no way I could continue or survive. Labour would either have to stop, or I felt I would die! It is so strong and takes over, and seeing the baby come into fruition is what you are living for. And then it came; not birthing, but breakthrough, a temporary reprieve! The breakthrough came at work through the slightest and most random of moments: a funny mispronunciation of a word which triggered off holy laughter with another of the students, which just continued to break over us both like waves. I knew my afternoon was wrecked, and as I yielded to the lightness, relief and long-awaited refreshing of His sweet spring rains, worship opened up in the office. Soaking led to more layers of breakthrough and by lunchtime I could barely function. The pressure and the pain which had been building over the past few weeks and was so intense in the morning had suddenly gone. My burden in prayer had been air-lifted and the skies were blue again. I found myself later in a nearby café, prophesying over people and releasing breakthrough over them. We ended up enjoying the new wine and freedom together and laughter rang from me like a peal of bells. All the heaviness had passed and I left feeling that I was beginning to see, by the mercy of God, people radically awakened and released as sons, following Jesus wherever He called and whatever the cost. (April 2013)

Whilst I am praying, as well as the Holy Spirit anaesthetic—a holy drug-relief from the pain of contractions resulting in peace, joy, drunkenness, a floaty feeling and loss of physical control!—God often sends me 'midwives' in the natural realm to help me push through and birth the long-awaited vision or breakthrough. They will literally sit by my side and talk me through it, holding my hand and encouraging me!

Light burdens?

When God asks you to hold something of His heart, it's important to learn not to bear the weight on your own. For me, intercession has a rhythm where you hear, feel or hold something of God and then release it back to Him, rather than being crushed by the seriousness of it or by false responsibility. Jesus Himself is interceding so it's necessary to release the burden to Him. It might help to visualise the person or issue with Jesus in heaven, or to take that person or situation to the cross. Jesus dealt with it there along with all sickness, sorrow, death and pain.

God has begun to show me His heart and call me to pray about prostitution and trafficking in this country. The reality of this stuff has hit me. I have revelation overload. I feel sick, stunned, like I am in shock. It is like God has just overturned a huge stone and now lots of stuff is suddenly scuttling around. I feel painfully aware of the injustice and my frustration. It's just so unfair. I cry and writhe and want to hit, punch and scream. I want to be relieved of the pain of it, but I don't know how. I keep just feeling it physically and emotionally then giving it back to God. I want to hit myself. I can't keep still; it's painful, it's sick, it's enormous and I am totally in shock that it is reality. Journaling gives me the hope of releasing it. I want to chat to someone who gets it. I so want to be relieved of it. I feel numb, ill. I keep clenching my fists, I feel heartbroken. It is so uncomfortable. (February 2013)

There have been times when I have felt the Father heart of God and He has led me to lament in prayer over a city. When I carry the heart of God for geographical areas, cities or nations, He will usually give me insight into some of the barriers and issues in that area and use me to bring breakthrough. Even though these burdens don't necessarily feel light, God provides ways for us to not become overwhelmed. Our prayers should not get stuck in the wrong place; we should not be praying out of fear or from an earthly perspective, but from the third realm. We don't focus on the work of the enemy or the effects 'on the ground', but we stand before the Father and ask, "What are you doing?"

Authority

Jesus is our model for prayer. He seemed to have two main ways of praying. The first was when he withdrew to a secluded place to be with His Father. He was alone and went to places He knew He wouldn't be disturbed. He also went at the times he was likely to have a long, uninterrupted audience with God: in a boat; climbing a mountain; kneeling in a quiet spot in the garden away from His friends; pilgrimage; retreat. Here He went to pour out His heart, to be restored and to seek wisdom before making decisions. This is the quiet place, the place of oneness, intimacy and privacy. He would emerge later with revelation for decision-making, with the courage needed for obedience or strengthened for ministry.

Out of this place of connection and centrality with God and whilst He was interacting with other people and revealing the Kingdom of God, we see the second type of prayer. As Jesus did the work of His Father—healing, raising the dead and casting out demons—He did not address the Father or beseech Him for help. He did not use formulas or lengthy wordy prayers. He just took authority and in simple sentences addressed the problem. He told it to go—'Get up!' 'Get out!' 'Be healed!'—or addressed the person and proclaimed the truth.

I was really challenged by this prayer model, but it honestly is as simple as this to follow Jesus in His ways. We allow ourselves to be aware of the activity of the Father in heaven and we simply speak or sing it in. God calls the things that are not as if they were (Romans 4:17). The Father gave Jesus authority and Jesus then gave *us* full authority to rule and reign, re-establishing the call on the first man, Adam. Increasingly, we can know the character of the kingdom and release the reality of it on earth. There is a shift from spiritual reality to earthly reality. "Your Kingdom come on earth, as it is in heaven." God brings created order into chaos after the Spirit broods over the earth and He simply speaks life. If you haven't tried praying this way before, give it a go; you may find it disarmingly simple and effective! Often my best prayer is this one: "Yes!" or "Amen;" my one-word prayer of agreement with what Daddy God is about to do next.

God showed me that in this time of shaking and shifting in this nation, we will win cities, streets and brothels by simply speaking truth about who God is. (January 2009)

Spiritual attack

Sometimes the enemy will come to oppose or steal God's work. We need to keep our eyes on Jesus rather than getting distracted and focussing on our enemy who has already been defeated. Perhaps speak out scripture—this is what Jesus did whilst being tempted in the wilderness—and remind yourself of the goodness and promises of God. Play worship and sing, dance or pray around the house; worship puts your eyes back on God and not on your circumstances. You have been given authority over the areas you live and work in. If something is going on in your house, your marriage, your children, your street or your church, rather than allowing your enemy to rampage all over it, you can come into agreement with heaven over it and enjoy the reality of God's goodness.

If you sense the enemy coming against you, bringing accusation or telling lies, you can simply rebuke him like Jesus did—'Get behind me satan!' 'Get lost!' or whatever admonishment feels appropriate—and receive and declare truth in its place. As satan cannot stand God's presence, the best way to combat spiritual attack is simply to spend time with Papa,

Daddy God, and our enemy will not be able to come anywhere near us. Standing in truth does not need to be complicated. We can rest whilst seeking strength and safety in the arms of our protector-restorer God until the storm passes. Worship and adoration will drive satan away.

Warfare

Warfare is a grand-sounding word for standing in truth. It is simple and habitual for those who know their position in God as sons and daughters. You simply live out a series of choices to hold onto truth and reject lies. This may need to be a conscious practice at first, but it will soon become a subconscious part of everyday life. Knowing truth is really important because it means that you don't need to receive that which is not true. Our feelings are not the same as truth, and although sometimes we cannot feel God's presence, the truth is that He is always there.

When God shows you something in the spiritual realm, He is showing you how it is meant to be in the natural realm. Coming into agreement with this truth through speaking it out, singing, drawing or just walking in it is a powerful thing.

A few years ago I was at a conference. In the privacy of my own thoughts, I asked God what my keys to warfare and breakthrough were. Within an hour, a stranger at the conference came up to me and asked, "Do you know what your keys are?" I was shocked, but I had a primal, emotional response that said, "Joy, worship and dance."

Over the years, I have recognised this as true. It doesn't mean that I am limited to these things, but I have known times when something has risen in me and I have found myself spontaneously dancing, laughing or singing over someone or some place. Knowing this has allowed me freedom to flow in these things because I know deep down that they are achieving something profound and unseen that I do not fully understand.

As well as a key to breakthrough, I am learning that worship is important in times of attack.

May the praise of God be in their mouths and a double-edged sword in their hands... to carry out the sentence written against them. (Psalm 149:6, 9a, NIV; received June 2003)

Listening to 'in spirit and in truth' worship is really liberating. There are times when I have been aware of sitting under a low-but-persistent level of oppression. Releasing an atmosphere of truth-filled worship can break such power without words, like sunshine piercing through a cloud.

For about ten years, I spent some time as a musical worship leader. I learnt the importance of worshipping in spirit and in truth and how it gives other people the freedom to praise God themselves and go to deeper levels with Him. As we worship, we give glory to God; we have an audience of One and it is all for Him. As we begin to focus on Him, it is we who change, not Him! He cannot get more magnificent, powerful or beautiful, but as we behold Him more and more, we become more like Him, the One we focus our attention and affection on. He comes, inhabits our praises and manifests His glory in the midst of us. How wonderful!

Watchmen

Watchmen (and women!) are those who are called to 'look out' from the heights of prayer and clear any enemy obstructions that could hinder the advancement of the Kingdom of God. They are essentially gatekeepers who guard entrances, responsible for being alert and determining who or what is allowed into our communities. We all have spheres of influence, places and communities where we have authority to reign, welcome Kingdom blessing and resist evil, like Adam in the first garden. For me, these areas include my home, family, marriage, friendships, my street, workplace, school, church, city and our country. What are yours?

Once we have heard the watchman call, we watch, wait and listen, standing in the gap and guarding the garden. Imagine that you are tending a beautiful plot. You want to encourage the plants and root out the weeds that will grow up and choke the plants if they're left unchecked. It is the same with watchman prayer. If something comes into your space which is not from God, you can break its power and uproot it in Jesus' name, then reclaim the space that the enemy tried to take.

Sometimes God may ask you to 'sound the alarm', to share what you have seen with others in the body of Christ, so that they are forewarned about the attacks of the enemy. Discernment is key here: God will give us insight, either through our senses or an intuition that something isn't right. The Bible tells us that even the devil can masquerade as an angel of light, which is why the role of the discerning sentry is so important.

And no wonder, for Satan himself masquerades as an angel of light. (2 Corinthians 11:14, NIV)

The other part of the role is to welcome in the purposes of God. Again, as we are watchful and susceptible to the direction the Holy Spirit, we might discern who God has sent as a messenger to bless and increase the Kingdom of God. As we watch in those high-up places, we can open the gates and usher in the blessings of God.

There are definitely seasons when I am more aware of operating as a watchman or sentry guard than others. If you feel like God is asking you to partner with Him in this way, report in for your assignment and ask Him to show you where and how to stand and watch. If you don't already have a trusted friend or group to pray with, ask Him whom you might join with. For nearly fifteen years I have prayed with another lady and we have seen God consistently heal, move mountains and do the seemingly impossible, time and time again. We are not to look at the problems from our own perspective, but to rise up and see what the Father sees and then pray and act accordingly. Praying in this way is not arduous, fruitless and dry, but exciting, adventurous, illuminating and effective. He always manifests

Himself in our midst, as He has promised to do as we gather to pray, and has guided us every step along the way as we seek to simply agree with His will. I thoroughly recommend it!

The Prophetic

I believe the prophetic is simply about hearing God, which means it's available for everyone. We can all prophesy, but this is different from being a prophet, which is a specific calling.

At the moment, there seems to be resurgence in the prophetic. I have noticed it particularly in evangelism: using words of knowledge; treasure hunting; prophetic art; healing on the streets. This is wonderful. As people step out in faith, they discover that God is already there; we simply join in with what He is already doing. The danger with the prophetic becoming 'trendy' is that it can be professionalised by a few 'experts', but the prophetic should be widespread, natural and normal. It comes out of a relationship with God. As you keep your eyes on God, continue to practice attending to that still small voice and take risks, your spiritual senses will become even more acute and you will find yourself taking off, beginning to fly, and soaring in Him.

It was about ten years ago that I decided to start attending to, and acting on, the voice of God in service of others. Often when I have a word from God to share, I feel very hot and as though my heart will jump out of my chest! Other people have told me they feel an 'unction' when they have something to share; the symptoms only go away once the message is delivered.

Although the prophetic is a gift, it can be trained like a muscle. Why not gather a few friends together and ask God for pictures or words for one another? The agreements and confirmations that follow as God shares His secrets with you will encourage you, I'm sure. Once hearing from God in this way becomes more natural, you can practice with people you don't know. Sitting on a train, shopping, walking down the street, at the gym; during the normal daily interactions we have, God can reveal information to us. He is keen to connect with those who do not know Him yet and encourage those who do. Keep your spiritual eyes and ears open and make yourself available, then it's likely to happen more and more.

There is a difference between being prophetic and having the role or mantle of a prophet. I believe that all of God's kids, saved and unsaved, have the ability to hear (and see) God speak and share it as a word in season to bless, build up and encourage. All genuine messages from God build up the person and lead them deeper into His purposes and the things of His kingdom. That doesn't mean that all prophetic words feel 'nice' and gentle; sometimes correction is necessary, but there is always a way back to God, to be restored completely to Him. In the Bible, the prophets often had difficult messages to deliver, but the purpose was always to turn the hearts of a people or nation back to God.

Being a prophet

As I have said, there is more to the role of a prophet than simply being prophetic. It is a specific calling to speak to people on behalf of God, serving as an intermediary between humanity and the divine. It is significant and not to be taken lightly. There is often a great cost involved in being a prophet. It requires obedience, trust and an emptying of self.

My experience of this role is that it feels like being a surrogate for something of God. The message becomes part of you as you stand in the gap between God and people. You have to learn to carry it in the right way, protecting and incubating it, until God says it is time for it to be released. A prophet must hear clearly what God is saying and release it at the right time. We mustn't try and give the message our own interpretation, change its substance or try and make it more palatable; the prophet is a hollowed-out vessel who will obediently hatch and dispatch the message.

Although partnering with God in this way is a rewarding adventure, it can also feel very uncomfortable. You may be one step ahead of the church, yearning for breakthrough. You might be at odds with both the church and the world, but you've seen what lies ahead and are being called to prepare the way. I often find that when I am weeping, everyone around me is laughing, but when I am celebrating and thanking God for the breakthrough, everyone around me is on their knees and crying out to Him. This is the role of the prophet: to make a pathway for our God; levelling the ground; bringing down the high and lofty places and raising up the humble and weak.

A final word on the subject of prophets. A major issue that you might have to deal with, because of the isolated path you may walk, is the fear of rejection. Beware of this, hold it before God and ask Him to refine you by fire. Don't attempt to bypass or avoid God's refining. When you are touched by the holiness of God, your words will carry true purity and their prophetic power will hit the target without compromise.

I was once worshipping with a friend, and the atmosphere quickly became thick with the glory of God. I saw an army; not one rallying for war, but one of immense purity and devoted hearts. As we slowly advanced, the enemy was pushed back in equal measure. Purity is a key vehicle for the prophet's message and it cannot be obtained cheaply. Allow the fire of God to consume you and the glory of God will be your rear guard.

Leadership

Leadership can take many forms. Usually church leadership is predominantly male, ordained and extrovert. I have found it difficult and painful being a woman who leads but is not called to recognised, ordained leadership. I had to learn that God was calling me to the very edges of the system, sometimes out of it, to those who are hungry for the deep things of God, whether they might be 'in' or 'out' of the established church. I have had to learn to lead on my knees, to follow Christ and walk humbly with Him whether anyone notices or not, to honour Him and His beautiful presence above all else. It means to choose righteousness and truth; to not be aligned to the plans of men and to live out a simple gospel. I have had to learn to embrace the narrow path, not compare myself to others and stay close and true to God, wherever He takes me.

This brings its own challenges and I can feel lonely at times, but we are not alone. As tragic as it might feel, if you are feeling lonely, ask God for a companion or group from whom you can draw strength, especially if it is not easy to express God authentically and freely in your normal gathering place.

Good leaders release others. They don't claim ownership of the things of God, but see who He is preparing and equip and release them, even (or especially) if it means their juniors running further and higher than themselves. Recognising new leaders comes by the Spirit. Sometimes I walk into a room and can feel or see something begin to bubble up inside someone that needs releasing. Other times, God has given me a word of knowledge. Don't just look for the 'next big thing', but look with upside-down 'kingdom eyes' and watch God point out those whose hearts are ready, available and teachable.

The leaders I most admire are those who have managed to walk lightly because they have a relationship with Jesus. They keep their youthfulness and sense of humour and are not alarmed when storms come. Their words bring life and their lives are centred on worship of Him. Because they have learnt that ministry is who they are rather something they do, they have allowed God to shape their character. They have gloriously deep roots. They are real about their difficulties and shortcomings because they don't need to prove themselves. Many have families, but have not sacrificed them on the altar of ministry. Being with them is always encouraging because the life of Christ constantly bubbles up from deep within them. I pray for more leaders like this to emerge.

Pioneering

There have been times when God has asked me to pioneer something new, both in the spiritual and natural realms. Pioneering can take many forms: sometimes being (manifesting something new of God), sometimes doing (starting a new work). In the former, you are a visionary who pioneers and your role is to see the new thing and pray it in as God leads. Then you can release it. Pioneering comes out of relationship and intimacy with God, not business models or five-year project plans.

The other side of pioneering is when you allow God to develop something in you which you then carry. When He shows you how, you simply release it. It's a call to be and allow the Kingdom to spread, rather than to found a new work.

For some years now, I have been carrying a manifestation of the presence of God and an intimate and experiential revelation of God and His kingdom. As I have mentioned elsewhere, for years I was the only person I knew of who shook in the presence of God, got 'lost' in Him and experienced His glory and heavenly realities so regularly, tangibly and deeply. At times, I've had the privilege of imparting this to others, resulting in their greater intimacy with God, boldness to do miracles, an explosion in creative gifts, the ability to 'see' in the Spirit, gifts of intercession, an impartation of God's heart for the lost, the impetus to pioneer, new levels of joy and freedom, the removal of idols and restoration of God as first love, a new desire for the presence and glory of God, recognition of sonship and destiny, leadership and pilgrimage.

So, here are some brief thoughts about pioneering, brought either by the Holy Spirit or mistakes and wrestling (or both). Firstly, Jesus only did what He saw the Father doing. The temptation is to 'make things happen', but He is the Saviour, we are not. This frees us to rest, hear from God and not get exhausted, frustrated or proud.

Secondly, guard against getting busy and carrying burdens which God has not asked us to carry. Being over-busy fills our lives and minds and makes discernment trickier. It lures us towards self-reliance and away from simply sitting at His feet. So, get into that secret place, wait for Him and hear His voice. God will increase our faith to continue to believe what we have been shown, no matter how our circumstances look.

Finally, once God has spoken, you need to stand on and activate His word. Don't wait for endless confirmations or allow your circumstances to limit your faith. If God has said, "Go!" then all that you need will be there when you need it. Don't try to rationalise what God is saying: His word is supernaturally inspired, so what is needed will be supernaturally supplied.

Chapter 9
Signs and wonders

Jesus moved in signs and wonders and so did His first disciples. They were trained by the Master and learnt by going out and having a go. They would come back, ask Him questions and understand more about how to move in God's power. Even before Jesus' sojourn on earth, we see the Godhead working in signs and wonders all the way through time. Creating stuff through words is the first miracle we see; good job God! We see Him speaking in dreams, sending angels as messengers, talking though animals and non-believers, conspiring to bring couples together, making babies thrive in old and barren wombs, making fires appear and waves part, bringing clouds of His glory, winning a public power contest against a shed-load of deities, saving people from immediate danger, giving ordinary people extra-ordinary insight and knowledge and healing and saving lives. And that's just the start. Throughout time, followers who have befriended this Jesus find themselves doing amazing exploits and having similar adventures. Why? These signs lead somewhere: they point to the reality of a relationship with a living and loving God whom we can know as individuals. Where there are genuine signs and wonders, there is the Kingdom, salvation and a glimpse of the new-creation order.

Words of knowledge

Words of knowledge are thoughts, pictures or just a sense of 'knowing something' that could only have been revealed to you by the Spirit of God. Sometimes these are to be prayed into and at other times, in the right *kairos* moment, they are to be shared. Normally their purpose is to reveal more of the Kingdom of God's reality to someone.

I will often know of a stranger's personal situation, grief, physical pain, desires, destinies, preferences or hobbies. When you are able to approach someone and demonstrate the reality and nearness of God by sharing the knowledge that has been imparted to you, it is a very powerful part of their healing, conversation, restoration or conversion.

I long to see followers of God mature in these gifts. I believe God wants to join His 'super-' to our '-natural' every day. So, if you feel you only have part of a message or picture, keep asking God questions until greater clarity or an interpretation comes. Then it is important to hold it before Him and wait to deliver the message until He indicates it needs to be shared. Have you ever been given a word from God and delivered it at exactly the right time? It's a life-giving word in season, a message that's like an arrow that hits the bullseye.

If you receive a word of knowledge from someone else and it speaks into your situation and lines up with the word and His nature, then it's clearly right. If you hear something which doesn't immediately make sense, don't reject it outright; maybe journal it and hold it lightly. If it *is* from God, you will see it fulfilled in time; if not, you won't!

You don't have to receive words if they don't feel right. There have been many times when I've seen the prophetic used as a form of control. It causes huge confusion when people have been connected for longer than they should to a person or situation because they have received and stood upon a word which wasn't accurate or Godly. If someone has forcibly and repeatedly told you that they are going to marry you, minister with you or walk closely with you for a season, and you haven't heard that for yourself that from God, you shouldn't feel any pressure to respond to, agree with or partner with them in any way. The prophetic can be abused, and words can be idols and snares wielded with intent to control instead of being life-giving and kingdom-building. Remain close to God. Be free to move only when He says so. If this has happened to you, be at peace. You know His voice and you hear Him. Just rest in Him, give Him the situation and ask for His protection and peace.

Sometimes God will give you a word of knowledge for someone by giving you a pain or sensation in the area of your body which God wants to heal in the other person. So, if you suddenly feel a pain which doesn't belong to you, ask Him who it is for. Then you can approach that person and (for example) simply ask, "Excuse me, are you struggling with a shooting pain in your arm? I think God wants to heal you today. Do you mind if I pray for you?"

Before I went to sleep, I began to pray for a friend and suddenly got a sharp pain in my rib area. It was so sharp and intense that I could hardly sit up! I prayed into it for a while, sensing she had received an impact through someone's words to her which had affected her spiritually and emotionally. Then the rib-pain left when the impetus to pray diminished. I called her the next day and she told me that was exactly what had happened. She had sustained a verbal wound from a fellow believer, and it had felt like she had been 'stabbed in the heart'. God knew, and had me pray for her; He is such an incredible communicator! (January 2013)

Physical Healing

I have desired the gift of healing for a long time. Up until about six years ago, I had never prayed for anyone to be healed—I probably thought that healing was the restricted domain of church leaders and healing evangelists. Whilst studying evangelism at the Light Project where I work, I was repeatedly drawn to a book about John Wimber. I had never heard of 'power evangelism' before, but I decided to study Wimber because I felt God wanted to speak to me about how He wanted to use me in evangelism in the future. I was gobsmacked as I read about how God gave Wimber the courage and anointing to pray for people to be healed and to bring words of knowledge as ways to close the gap between God and man.

So, I began to step out, hungry to see the Kingdom of God advance in this way. I had not yet discovered what evangelism would look like for me in practice, but I was sure that what I had read about would be a key part of it. I literally began to practice on people. I would pray for dozens of people, but at first there was little change. I felt discouraged, but then remembered that Wimber had prayed for *hundreds* of people before he saw healing breaking out. Even during this time of waiting, he would take teams of people out to perform healings: what bravery and humility!

God trained me on the job and I began to find simple ways to pray for people which felt comfortable to me. I learnt not to pray on my own for someone of the opposite gender and I learnt to keep my eyes open as I prayed for people to watch for signs of God moving. I would normally ask the person about the problem whilst listening to the Holy Spirit to see if there was an underlying issue or root cause of the pain or disease. I would also ask them if there was anything else they would like prayer for; sometimes the pain linked to an issue they were struggling with. I might ask permission to lay my hands on them, to just lightly touch them on the shoulder or at the perceived site of the pain (as long as it was in an area that was appropriate to touch!). Some people would rather you prayed for them later rather than right there; others prefer you not to lay hands on them. It is really important to respect their wishes in this area. It's their body, their personal space and their time; we do not display the character of Jesus effectively if we are rude, pressurising or intimidatingly persistent. Jesus Himself offered the rich young ruler a way into the Kingdom and had to let him walk away; people have a choice and must always be free to make it.

In terms of what prayers to pray, I would always try and pray as directed by God. In more straightforward situations, I would simply tell the pain to leave in Jesus' name and invite the healing presence of God's Spirit. Then you can ask what's happening or how they physically feel and pray as their responses lead. I have discovered that prayer for healing can be multi-faceted, so we really must listen to His still, small voice during the process. I have also learned to trust more in the unseen than the seen when it comes to physical healing. Whilst it's important to ask the person you're praying for what they're experiencing and seeing, there may be something different or unexpected that God wants to do first (or instead). Physical sickness can be caused by many things: trauma; curses; unforgiveness; something generational. It's important to be listening to the Holy Spirit as you go along and I am often prompted to pray for emotional healing, touching a sadness or hurt, first.

Someone came to me for prayer for healing because she was anxious and struggling to sleep. God showed us that these things originated from abuse she had suffered, so we prayed into that. Since we prayed, she reports that she now has no fear or animosity. She has complete release and her daily nightmares and flashbacks have stopped. (September 2009)

There were many times where the person I was praying for felt heat or a tingling sensation where my hands were laid on them, which then spread through their whole body. I normally take this as an encouraging sign that God's healing power is at work. Sometimes, people described the pain reducing but not leaving completely; I learnt that I could pray again, taking authority in Jesus' name, and tell *all* the pain to leave; often it would.

One time, I was praying for a young woman who had pains in her knee. With her permission, we laid hands on her and prayed at the site of the pain, but it didn't go. I felt we should ask her what caused the pain in the first place (i.e. what the root cause was); He began to surface memories and hurts about her parents' divorce. She began to pray and release forgiveness over her pain and rejection; the pain in her knee began to move. I 'saw' that it would move down her leg and exit through her toes; when we prayed in Jesus' name for it to leave, it did.

According to scripture, Jesus was never sick. I had that revelation whilst I was reading about John Wimber and I found it astounding. I am sure that if Jesus had been poorly or had needed healing, it would have been significant enough to record in the scriptures. I realised that sickness is not for us and I began to refuse it if it came my way. I have often woken up with a headache or feeling sick and told it to go away and it has! At other times, I have prayed in this way and it hasn't gone away. I struggle intermittently with insomnia and I get coughs, colds, aches and pains like everyone else, but we shouldn't accept these things as standard.

It has been an amazing and exciting privilege to see people being healed by God. Every time it's a thrill! I have seen limping people (and animals!) suddenly able to run, blind people able to see, people hunched in pain able to freely straighten up, babies being conceived against all medical hope and people with long term pain or sickness instantly relieved. I have seen people being supernaturally healed at work, in shops, on the streets, in gyms, in play centres, behind the checkouts, in hospital and at the school gates. It's really worth persevering with. It all comes through the unmerited grace of God and each healing is an opportunity to put Jesus on display and reveal more about the reality of a Kingdom with no sickness, suffering, pain, fears, separation, trauma or death. So, if you are stepping out to pray for healing, don't lose heart and give up; keep going, for His glory.

We had an amazing time today. We had hardly left our office when we encountered two guys. I had met one of them before when he came into our church, homeless and desperate. I had prayed for him that day, for a miracle, for safety, healing, provision and released destiny. When I saw him today, he told us his whole life had turned around since then and He had put it down to God. His friend was cynical so I asked him if we could pray for him. He had been in an accident when he was a teenager, causing him partial blindness in his right eye. You could see a white cloudy shape which obscured the colour of his pupils. We prayed simply, and after a minute or two, another team member exclaimed, 'Look at his eye!' We saw that the white shape had moved and his eye had returned to its normal colour. He freaked out as he checked his 'bad' eye because previously he could not make out objects at distance or at close range through it! This was the first creative miracle I had witnessed where you could clearly see the 'before' and 'after' changes and it blew us all away. (January 2011)

Sometimes it can be really powerful to get someone who has experienced healing to pray for others with that same complaint. Their faith is strong because they know beyond all doubt that God can heal in that way. I also love to see people who don't yet know Jesus praying for others in His name and seeing their shock as He answers their prayer and heals. Sometimes faith is significant in healing, but many times I have seen tiny mustard seeds be sufficient.

I have experienced God passing on an anointing or healing ability from one person to another. I was once at a conference, troubled by a friend's mental health episode. I asked a ministry lady for prayer for her. She took a piece of tissue, prayed for my friend, and told me to give it to her to put under her pillow, because the tormenting thoughts usually came at night. I wasn't sure about it at first, but I knew it had a Biblical basis and I was keen for a breakthrough. My friend slept with the tissue under her pillow and the symptoms gradually receded; she is now healthy and fully-restored in her mind. We shouldn't really be surprised at this: there is power in the name of Jesus! Sometimes I get a glimpse of this power: it's like an off-the-scale net that casts far and wide.

If there is an area which you want to grow in, go and find someone who is already operating in this area. Spending time, hanging out together, can really bring understanding of who you are and the new thing God is showing you. If you sense it's God's will, you can ask Him to transfer and spread that supernatural ability.

Emotional healing

A lot is said about physical healing, but for a long time I had not understood that God wants to heal deeply and emotionally too. He is holistic, concerned about the whole person: body, mind, emotions, circumstances and spirit. Only He can reach in and touch the things that are locked away in the past, before we were born, in our subconscious or in our buried and forgotten memories. If we open these areas up to God and invite Him into the whole lot, totally surrendered, He may begin to reveal our memories. We might even feel them there and then, as if we were experiencing them for the first time, only this time we are experiencing them in the safe embrace of God.

It is true that when we are born from above as new creations, we are no longer bound by our old behaviours. Nevertheless, we have all been brought up in a fallen world and those things continue to affect our identity, behaviour and choices to a greater or lesser extent. If we have been emotionally or physically wounded or have experienced trauma, we can become fractured, where we continue to grow but within us there remains a child stuck at that point of vulnerability. Once that inner child (or children) experiences healing, wholeness pervades the whole person.

We should avoid focussing on the past and delving backwards unless God leads us this way, but if He does, don't be scared! He was there; He has a purpose for you and you are not a mistake. He knows what has affected us and with the best will in the world, our parents were not perfect. Others around us may have hurt us or let us down as well. We may need healing from those hidden, unconscious thoughts and actions from long ago.

God began to minister to me and show me that I was trying to sanitise myself and only show Him the good, the acceptable and the presentable. I was telling Him it was too messy to show Him and He showed me the cross: messy; lonely; bloody; painful; protracted; shockingly horrific. He deals in mess and broken lives, that's His currency. I felt very emotional, like I am in mourning, very empty and needing filling, laid bare, exposed, laid out, like a lab rat or a flower opened out with the petals gently pinned down. Surely I can cry no more. I am on the threshold of the old and the new. (January 2008)

We need to be aware of this when ministering to others. We should listen to God and watch the person to see what the Holy Spirit is doing. As well as the demonic, the person may have fractured or dissociated parts inside them resulting from pain or trauma. These parts might have their own personalities and speak or manifest. Someone who has experienced a lot of trauma may have many different personalities. We can do more harm than good if we assume that when someone 'switches' and begins to speak with a different voice or in a different character, the source is demonic and needs to be quietened or cast out. The Holy Spirit will show us how to minister in these situations; no 'how-to' manual exists, but He is the comforter and healer. These situations are not yet commonplace within church prayer ministry, but I believe that God will help us to understand these things better as we get more involved in the brokenness and messiness of the world.

If you recognise that you may need this emotional healing, open yourself up to God. Invite Him, in His timing and His way, to bring you the healing you need. We don't need to be frightened or unsure of what He might do; He is love, He is the healer, He is the restorer, He is the comforter. These are His names and He never acts out of character. So, submit your scars to heaven's love and watch what He does.

Gifts and provision

I know many people who have lived whole lives without regular income. They see God provide financially for them time and time again, enough for their needs and just in time. God has not only provided finances miraculously, but also clothes and food; and not just sparsely, but generously and according to exact need, size and personal taste! I learnt to let God know of every need, even the little things, and He always provided. It's happened with money and food as well, time and time again. These things are a faith-growing sign—not only for us, but also for others who witness and observe our lives—that God is in the business of acting powerfully, generously, specifically and just in time.

Becoming a sign and a wonder

Many Christians want to *do* signs and wonders, but will people respond to His wooing and *become* a sign and a wonder? John the Baptist was a sign, and so were undignified David and many of the prophets. The Christian mystical realm is by invitation only. If you are invited there, you need to be prepared to go alone, as it is a secret place where mysteries are revealed and what is hidden becomes seen. To yield to Him alone has meant saying goodbye to friends and being thought of as 'no earthly use'. These things are painful to the flesh! I am still learning lessons, some the hard way. I have yearned for wider community, for companions along the journey, but there are some places you can only go to alone. Sometimes God is doing something so unusual that there is no one to connect with because your experience is unique. Many worries have had to be dealt with in order to keep progressing deeper into the things of God. What will people think of me?! How will this work with me being the wife of a Church of England clergyman? Will I ever come back to earth?! Will I be able to work? How will the money come in?

Being a sign and a wonder means that instead of *reading* the message, you *become* the message. Like Ezekiel, you have eaten the scroll; the word is deep within you. As you live and move, you flow in the Spirit and signs and wonders occur naturally. We cease to become people who *sometimes* do miracles or are anointed for the prophetic or leading worship; instead we become people who operate in the fullness of the Spirit of God *all the time*. We operate less in our heads and become more instinctive, intuitive and flowing, grafted in to heaven and creation.

At times, God will use people who are signs and wonders as an offence to the church. I have heard one person describe themselves as 'the grit in the pearl'. They are like that family member who is embarrassing, loud and unyielding. We wish they would quieten down and sit sensibly in the corner! Church 'performance' has much to do with good behaviour and outward demonstration, so when God brings in someone who doesn't follow suit, it is very revealing of people's hearts. Those who are offended by God's messengers are ultimately offended by Him. His word makes it clear that He uses the foolish to confound the wise. Our wisdom is not the same as His wisdom.

> *But God chose the foolish things of the world to shame the wise; God chose the weak things of the world to shame the strong.*
> (1Corinthians 1:27, NIV)

Many times, people have spoken over me that the ministry my husband and I will be involved in will be controversial. One lady even said that I will be much misunderstood because things will happen that are beyond even what was experienced and accepted in previous revivals. These words are daunting, but I know even as I write this book that the things I have experienced so far may only be the tip of the iceberg compared with what's to come.

If you find yourself offended or in contention with something which is going on around you, try not to judge it against the limitations of your own understanding. Simply ask God, "Is this you?" If he says no, keep your heart soft and pray for them, bless them and move on. If He confirms it is Him, you may need to say sorry for not recognising Him and judging your brothers and sisters. It might be permissible for you too: be open to God moving in you as well. It will be glorify Him and be good for your soul!

Friends of ours laugh with us now because I once refused their invitation to pray for a 'refreshing' for me after God had done some in-depth inner healing. I was so fearful, prideful and in control. Eventually I was so desperate for the presence of God that I no longer cared what happened or how it looked to others. Death to self and refining are both wonderful tools that God may deploy along the way to deal with our hearts and bring us into glorious freedom in Him. I want to encourage you to be a highly infectious carrier, to stay in the fire and be poured out for others. It's magnetic and draws people to God.

I recognise a call to something that looks reclusive, ridiculous, monastic, radical, dangerous, unsavoury, overflowing, and associating with the least. Lord, will this expose me as a mad revolutionary prophet, speaking out where you have called me to smash walls down? Or will I retreat in peace and live out a totally different life, for people to see or not, at your pleasure? Like the Mona Lisa, smiling inside, all is well. At this stage, I have no idea. But I know there is no way back. (January 2013)

There are a few things I have learnt recently which have helped me to be a signpost and a wonder. Firstly, sometimes it may feel as if you are 'in' and at other times as if you are 'out' of the Spirit, but the truth is that you are 'in' all the time. You can choose to draw back from it when you need to, unlike the hypnotism or mind-control which people come under in other spiritual practices. Knowing this is reassuring when we feel apprehensive about where this journey might take us.

Secondly, I would advise you to spend time with people who know you well and will love you unconditionally. These people should have the maturity and grace to say, "Whilst this is not my experience, I know you love God and I can see good fruit. I will walk with you, cheer you on, not judge you and allow God to be bigger than my knowing and comprehension". Learning to release in God's timing what you are carrying requires His gifts and grace to help you perceive what is going on. Don't shrink back from asking Him and others for the help you need. What you are carrying is needed by the body and healing balm for the lost.

Mission

Before I close this chapter on signs and wonders, I want to say something about mission. Jesus only did what He saw His Father doing. He responded to but was not overwhelmed or wearied by the needs around Him. We must learn to do the same, especially if we are particularly sensitive, empathic or have a seer gift. I have often think of Mother Theresa, who when asked how she ministered to so many, answered, "One by one." I have learnt, sometimes the hard way, that there is beauty in the one-by-one.

I really identify with D.T. Niles' definition of evangelism as, 'one beggar helping another beggar to find bread.' Evangelism is not doing something *to* somebody, it's journeying together to taste more of the goodness of God. Mission is not an event or an outreach, it's a lifestyle, an overflow of our fullness in Him. Imagine you are a cup, hollowed out by Jesus. The more you yield to Him, the more He fills you. Whatever is in you will overflow. If this is goodness, peace, love and joy, then you won't be able to stop those fruits spilling out and splashing everyone. In other words, be full and just overflow. This means that mission, evangelism, loving or whatever you want to call it will look different in different people. Some will share love, others will serve practically, some will teach, others will give money, some will be called to the workplace, others to itinerant ministry. Just learn who you are, be smeared and filled with God and then overflow.

Often, the heart of God will take you further to the edge and you will find yourself emboldened to do things you never imagined you could. Caring for people with hectic, complex and multi-layered lives calls needs us to be fully rooted in Christ, so don't be surprised if you find that God takes you deeper into Him before you reach further out. It is imperative that we yield to these times. We should also personally practice good spiritual hygiene when caring for those who have been neglected. Operating out of forgiveness, not holding offence, allowing God to cleanse and refresh us and walking lightly and in grace will protect our emotional, spiritual and physical wellbeing.

Revival

As far as I understand it, when we call out to God for revival, we are asking Him to move in power amongst the church and to awaken his bride to its identity, place and purpose so that they go into the world empowered by the Holy Spirit. God moves in undeniable power, turning the hearts of people towards Him in miraculous ways so that they fall under his power and come to faith. Those who pray, "God, send revival!" are often used as the first fruits of revival. They have their lives and priorities turned upside down as they ask for God to move: revival begins in them first and then snowballs out.

I often 'see' what this might look like. Space is made for God to be God, Jesus is desired, loved and honoured in both the church and the world, and the Kingdom becomes an earthly reality. People are set free and their lives are turned around and re-ordered from the inside out. The fruits of the Spirit overflow into relationships, marriages, communities, and businesses. People grow quickly in their faith; the broken ones who are saved and healed today become leaders and spiritual parents tomorrow.

It's probably contentious in the church at present to pray for revival. Some speak of needing such refreshment at a time when the church is served-out and surrounded by a dry and parched land. Others suggest that we shouldn't ask for revival when we already have the fullness of Christ living inside of us; to ask for 'more' doesn't make sense. Critics of revival suggest that the fruit is short-lived and that the meetings owed more to hype than divine visitation; those who responded to an altar-call for salvation never came into a living relationship with God and therefore the lasting fruits were few. However, I have also spoken to people who are direct descendants of those touched by previous revivals. Lasting transformation occurred and was passed down from generation to generation. That revival fire still inhabits their DNA and without it, they wouldn't be living radical, God-surrendered lives. Duncan Campbell, speaking about the Hebridean revival in 1945, described a "community saturated with God"[4] which resulted in conversions, baptisms, holiness, miracles, healings, liberation from darkness, crime reduction, broken addictions, restored marriages, realigned social structures and strengthened communities. When God genuinely moves in power, the fruit lasts and ripples down through many generations.

I guess we each have to respond as God directs us. For me, I long to see Jesus renowned, people converted, lives transformed, lifestyles changed, homes and families healed, *ekklesias* packed out and beautified and individuals on fire with zeal for God. If that needs revival, then so be it! We are seeing small fires start and wells open up, but I don't think we have seen anything like the fullness and extent of God's glory. I want to see so much more and I think it's needed, so I *do* ask repeatedly for more of God's Spirit, I *do* ask for the church to be refreshed and I *do* ask Jesus to come back again soon. Particularly in the last few years, I feel the longing of creation and the birth-pangs of a quickening and a response to the invitation of God to pray. Join me in this prayer if you dare: "Send revival and start with me!"

Following the cloud

I believe we are currently living in a time of transition where some of the old structures are disintegrating and God is building the new alongside them. Man-built church may indeed be dying out, but yet His Church, His bride, is rising up and taking flight like a fiery phoenix; the fire of resurrection power is being stoked in the *ekklesia*. Many will claim to have the 'key', the kernel of revelation or the pivotal 'golden ticket' which will see us through in these times. But we mustn't camp here; this is base camp. Even if we know Him intimately, we have only really glimpsed Him or sipped of Him. We can go up higher and there is no summit. Be suspicious if the unique selling point or the crux of the matter is anything other than Him and Him crucified. Angels, portals, gemstones, heaven, grace, organic church, healing, the prophetic, the mystical movement, manifestations, power evangelism, drunkenness, monasticism, missional community, radical liberty or whatever new revelation or ministry may be good in and of themselves, but we cannot focus our life on any one of them. Each will leave us wanting, gasping. They are signposts to Him, but only He can satisfy.

There are times when we cannot 'find' God's presence in the places we used to find it. We need to follow the cloud, to tarry for it, to search Him out and to know Him wherever and however He appears. If we have a box which God normally fits in—when I play this anointed CD, this normally happens; I hope it's 'X' leading worship today; if only I could get to 'Place X', then I could get an impartation from 'X'—we may find He wants to reveal Himself in a new way. He is not some slot machine, whose inputs and outputs are predictable. *Nothing* can hold Him in. So, there are times when we have to retreat and recover that deep place of knowing where we leave the crowd to follow the cloud. There are places I go to where people are still doing the same routine, putting the coin in the slot machine and doing their dance, but they have failed to notice that God is not playing. He will not perform; He has withdrawn His manifest presence. Our purpose is to know Him as He is, know His presence and when He says so, move out from our positions to follow it.

It is awesome when God reveals Himself in these new ways and places. He is so much bigger than we first thought! Sometimes I discover Him afresh in lots of different ways in just a single day: first in intimacy, then in joy, then in awe and then again in tenderness. When Jesus entered the world with skin on, many didn't recognise Him, even though they (the Pharisees) knew about Him and had studied Him. Later, some travelled with him on the road to Emmaus as friends, but didn't know Him, even though they were walking and talking with Him. I long to be someone who recognises Him in whatever form He manifests in. I don't want to be offended by Jesus, by God, by His presence or His glory when it comes! I want to recognise it, embrace it and beckon others to join in.

Chapter 10
Parting words

I hope you have enjoyed reading this book. It is simply an eye-witness account of part of a long stroll in the garden of life, with the divine. It was written to glorify Him, to testify to the power of our risen and ascended Jesus, to simplify the conundrum and to reveal some of the mystery.

There are no rules or methods by which any of His gifts, fruits, healings and salvations come other than by the initiation of the Spirit of God. His creativity is astonishing. It frequently fills me with bursts of joy and delight as He shows off His freedom to rule, establish and release in a myriad of different, surprising and colourful ways. He doesn't want us to follow a 'Ten-steps to...' ministry programme or the world's business models, or be narrowed and limited by duplicating the way He works through someone else. He wants us to walk with the Messiah, the Anointed One, the Sinless Offering, the One who was crucified and lifted up: Jesus.

Growing

Knowing Jesus intimately and loving Him radically means that you can't help but grow. I don't know what that will look like and neither do you. Bring your whole self to God, take His hand and see where the ride takes you. You may not have chosen your walk, your weapons or your destiny, but the present and the future with Him look distinctly better than any past without Him that you might have had. In each new season there will be more things to explore, more expansion, glory to glory and a whole new world to discover with Him.

Sowing

The scriptures clearly tell us, in figurative language and using various pictures, that it is God who waters when we plant a seed. We are to be those who sow, yet much of what we spend our time on in the established church is watering. We become addicted to ministry, we run discipleship groups, we hold home groups which follow the pattern of Sunday's sermon and we check new believers for signs of growth and sin-reduction. This keeps Christians in a milk-hungering, passive, pre-crawling, stunted development stupor, even those that have been in the faith for many years. We are effectively heaping our own judgements and patterns onto new believers. We make people dependent on us rather than on God Himself and we turn knowing God into a checklist of knowledge about God. We are so intent on watering—giving God a hand in case His water runs out—that the sowing stops!

Instead, let's sow wherever God puts us. Let what He has put in each one of us overflow, spilling seeds where we go and letting Christ's life be seen in us. We sow, He waters. Let's partner with Him in that and be faithful in planting whatever God has given you. Like David—the 'dragon-slayer'—just use whatever's in your hands. Don't try and be like someone else; their clunky ill-fitting armour will restrict you severely.

Knowing

I want to end this book as I began it. I thoroughly endorse Jesus Christ and commend Him to you as a person whom we can know and enjoy every day and for evermore. Perhaps as I describe different types of people below, you might recognise yourself. My prayer for you as you finish this book is that you will simply invite Him to reveal Himself to you more. Welcome the Holy Spirit. Ask the Father to pour out His love on you and He will show you what to do next.

Maybe you have never met Him or thought about Him before. You might have tried many other spiritual things. You might have had some similar supernatural experiences to mine, just not necessarily through Jesus. It is true that people can experience many of these things in other ways, but Jesus brings life in all its fullness and is the sure way to God. He is the gateway to true ecstasy, knowledge, fullness, freedom, love, power and the unveiling of mystery. The other ways lead to death. They can only imitate. They can't bring fullness of life; they just don't have the capacity to complete on the final transaction they first quoted you. They may promise much at first—even God-likeness, knowledge, miraculous and supernatural ability—but eventually the puppeteer, whatever or whoever that is, will cut the strings and you will find yourself plunged into deeper misery, sickness, fear and death than when you first began your quest. This language is not easy and as I write, I cringe a little at its directness, but I retain it here because I believe that the solution might bring you life. So, if you have got involved in anything which has taken over your life and want to know this Jesus for yourself and have Him rescue you from all cheap imitations, the first step is simple. God is bigger than any dabbling or full-on involvement in the supernatural, any addiction, any lifestyle or any pit you may feel it is impossible to leave. He can overcome them all. Simply call on the name of Jesus. Ask Him to save you. Ask Him to reveal Himself to you. Welcome the beautiful Holy Spirit I have been describing. Ask the Father to pour out His love on you. The ensuing journey might not be easy, but He will be with you and show you what to do next.

Perhaps you are reading this and feeling relieved, maybe even a bit proud, that you don't need de-tangling from difficult situations or your past. You might consider yourself already 'in'. You may have spent time developing thought, enjoying debate, gathering theological snippets, bolstering your arguments peppered with scripture about Jesus... but you don't know Him for yourself. If that's the case, you may be missing the whole point of what you are here for. All of those doctrines, knowledge and clever-sounding arguments will increasingly wrap themselves around you, constrict your breathing and take away your ability to live in the fullness we were created for. Leave that life behind and let someone else take up that mantle. I am sure there will be long queue of people willing to take your position of honour in the visible places. Come away and reacquaint yourself with Jesus. Why not commit to a new life of freedom and fullness? Simply receive and believe; read and reinterpret with fresh eyes. Be an encourager, lover, builder and adventurer of something way bigger than our little boxes. Come and be a child again; come and dream big dreams; use whatever colours you want to paint your picture. You can even go outside the lines... in fact, there are no lines! You can play. You are safe. You are free. You are loved. Simply call on the name of Jesus. Ask Him to save you. Tell Him you want to know Him. Invite the Holy Spirit to open your eyes, reveal Jesus and fill you. Ask the Father to take away all performance-related motivation and religion and allow Him to pour His love over you. This may be for the first time, or one of many, but drink deeply and stay there. Keep Jesus central and don't go back; cease doing the old things that made you feel righteous and follow Him, fully surrendered. He will show you what to do next.

Maybe you have read this book and don't want to know God at all. That could be because you don't connect with my experiences or my description of God's revelation and His work. If this is the case, don't allow my little glimpses of God or anything else to limit what your story could be. Ask Him, if He's real, to show you directly who He is Himself.

You may be someone who has been a Christian for a long time. Maybe you don't recognise the need for radical freedom, a change of direction or focus that I have suggested to other groups, yet you would like to experience more of what I have been speaking about. Whatever you have believed or experienced to the contrary, He wants to go deeper with you as much—if not more—than you do. He has already made the way. The Way is seated in heaven on a throne, and as I write this, I see Him, Jesus, patting the empty space next to Him on that big throne, winking and smiling at you and inviting you to come up to Him. "Come on, up you come!" Just believe and it is. Simply invite Him to reveal Himself to you more. Welcome the Holy Spirit. Ask the Father to pour out His love on you. He will show you what to do next.

Maybe you are a believer but disagree with things I have said. I know that feeling when you're really uncomfortable with something that's in front of you. Please don't be offended by anything I have written, but ask God if it's true and of Him. If His answer is 'no', then leave it. If His answer is 'yes', then allow Him to work in your heart, show you truth, bring you freedom and allow you to agree to His invitation to know Him more. He is good. He won't do anything which is bad; this is impossible for Him. I pray for His grace for you to ask that initial question, wisdom to hear His answer and yet more grace to enable you to respond.

You may have experienced all that I've described and more! Blessings on you! I ask God to take you higher, deeper and wider into His bounteous, limitless mystery and love. There's no ceiling, no walls and no floor. Simply invite Him to reveal Himself to you more. Welcome the Holy Spirit. Ask the Father to pour out His love on you. He will show you what to do next...

References

[1] *Common Worship: Services and Prayers for the Church of England,* copyright © The Archbishops' Council (2000)

[2] Iranaeus of Lyon, *Against Heresies*, Book IV Chapter 20

[3] Maloney, James (2011) *Ladies of Gold: The Remarkable Ministry of the Golden Candlestick*, Volume One, WestBow Press, A Division of Thomas Nelson, p33

[4] Edwards Brian H (2000) *Revival: A People Saturated With God*, Evangelical Press